Irony and Jesus:
Parables, Miracles and Stories

by
Rob Gieselmann

APOCRYPHILE
PRESS

THE APOCRYPHILE PRESS
Berkeley, CA
www.apocryphile.org

Copyright © 2019 by Rob Gieselmann
ISBN 978-1-949643-29-9 | paperback
ISBN 978-1-949643-30-5 | epub

All rights reserved. No part of this book may be reproduced or transmitted in any form or by any means, electronic or mechanical, including photocopying, recording or by an information storage and retrieval system without permission in writing from the publisher.

Translations Used:

The Scripture quotations contained herein are, except as noted below, from the New Revised Standard Version Bible, copyright 1989 by the Division of the Christian Education of the National Council of the Churches of Christ in the U.S.A., and are used by permission. All rights reserved.

*Th*e Scripture quotations marked "Jer." are taken from *The Jerusalem Bible*, copyright 1966 by Darton, Longman & Todd, Ltd. and Doubleday, a Division of Bantam Doubleday Dell Publishing Group, Inc. Reprinted by permission.

The Scripture quotations marked "NASB" are taken from the NEW AMERICAN STANDARD BIBLE, Copyright 1960, 1962, 1963, 1968, 1971, 1972, 1973,1975, 1977, 1995 by The Lockman Foundation. Used by permission.

The Scripture quotations marked "KJV" are taken from the Holy Bible, King James Version.

Dedication

For Reenie (1933-2018). A most extraordinary woman and mother who always found the kindness of grace tucked neatly within the words of Scripture.

Table of Contents

Prologue – Lessons from Crows:
   An Introduction to Murder.................................. 1

1. **Faith and Leaning into God**
   (or God's Leaning into You) 9
   Matthew 13: Parable of the Sower

2. **Walking on Water is Not Faith** 21
   Matthew 14: Jesus/Peter Walking on Water

3. **From each according to her abilities, to each**
   according to her needs (The Marxism of Jesus) 33
   Matthew 20: Parable of the Landowner

4. **The Blessings of a Man whose Friends are Good** 47
   Mark 2: Healing of the Man on a Pallet

5. **You Give them Something to Eat** 55
   Mark 6: Feeding the Multitude

6. **The Rudeness of Jesus** 65
   Mark 7: Syrophoenician Woman I

7. **Jesus Scandalously Opens the Communion Table to all** 77
   Matthew 15: Canaanite (Syrophoenician) Woman II

8. **What's in a Name?** 85
   Mark 12: Relation of Jesus to David, David to Jesus

9. **The Goo That is Faith** 97
   Luke 8: Jairus and the Woman with the Hemorrhage

10. **Would the Real Prodigal Please Stand Up?** 107
    Luke 15: The Prodigal Son I

11. **Jesus as Prodigal** 115
    Luke 15: The Prodigal Son II

12. **Good Friday: The Irony of the Cross** 121

Epilogue – Attention: Faith, hope and love. 127

Irony and Jesus
Parables, Miracles and Stories

Prologue

Lessons from Crows: An Introduction to Murder

They are offensive. Strategically perched at the tops of trees, crows *crow*, often about dangers that do not exist. They bully other birds unnecessarily, collaborate to steal eggs and kidnap hatchlings from the nests of finches and bluebirds. Even jays dart about fretfully when crows cycle through the neighborhood like a band of bikers. A gaggle of geese and a murder of crows, and you know that geese are called a gaggle because they gaggle like geese, while crows are called a murder because they commit first degree.

Perhaps these bullies should be called *a scavenge*. Gypsies, they scour loose garbage, pull apart fast food wrappers, scatter rotting fish and peck at decaying produce.

Ornithologists will try to convince you just how smart crows are. From tactical perches in tall trees, crows report neighborhood news to one another, cackling tales of murder and sharing secrets of new-found garbage. They build actual crows' nests where neighborhoods feel safe to them, and they avoid neighborhoods where danger threatens them.

Crows are not just mean, they are loud. Their cawing is a noise pollution that grates on nerves, like a murder of teenagers gossiping at the mall. I have been known to dart outside, lob small rocks at them (crows, not teenagers), and clap and yell to drive them away. I hope the crows sense danger in my neighborhood and pass this message across the treetops: *We must leave; we are not welcome here.*

Those same ornithologists who claim that crows are smart also assert that crows have an innate ability to distinguish human faces.

Crows, they say, recognize people as individuals. Good. I hope these pirates will recognize me and share my message of rejection with their entire murder: *This man is crazy. Let's go elsewhere.*

One delightful spring day, while still living in California, I was reading a novel on the back deck of our house that overlooks the Tiburon hillside. It was my day off, a Sabbath of timeless emptiness. The sun washed warm on my face, and I closed my eyes. Daydreamed. Feeling my own hopes and dreams, fears and fallibility, pulsing with each heartbeat. I opened my eyes. I read another page or two, then looked out on Mt. Tam off in the distance. The mystery and mastery appeared forest green.

I closed my eyes again and felt the goodness of the day. I breathed in, breathed out, breathed in, out. Now I drifted off, just shy of sleep, eyes again closed, when from my dreamlike states, I heard the faint yet intrusive crow of crows. They seemed agitated, though far away. I felt more than heard them, the murder flying towards me from the east, above the hill behind me. Their sound grew urgent, so I opened my eyes. As the murder approached me from behind, it divided into two flanks, one flying around the north side of the house and the other flying around the south side. The murder swooped down into the valley below, their cawing became – how shall I describe this? – *melliferous* – yet elegiac. Crows on either side of me now, their exquisite voices a symphony stereophonic, as though I was standing center stage surrounded by an orchestra playing Mozart's Requiem. Elegant and beautiful, dozens and perhaps several hundred crows raced past me in murderous pursuit.

The crows were mad as hell.

When they passed, I stood up to watch them fly to a neighbor's house in the valley below. A solitary pine tree stood in a distant neighbor's backyard. Some of the crows darted into the middle of the conifer, while most circled as vultures around it.

Why were the crows angry? I wondered. I found binoculars and tried to see whether there was something in the tree that drew their ire – which there was. A hawk, perched stoically on one of the pine's larger branches.

Crows and hawks are mortal enemies. They fight like kamikaze pilots in midair, as in duels to death. This particular murder of crows had cornered this lone hawk hoping to, I supposed, commit murder.

I became angry. The injustice – dozens against one – so I grabbed my car keys and raced downhill to intervene. I encountered the owner of the house, a woman I knew, and explained the situation to her.

"*I was curious why so many crows were hovering out back,*" she answered.

"*Do you have any idea why they came to your house?*" I asked. "*A hawk,*" I continued before she could answer. *I think the crows may have cornered a hawk in your tree and they want to kill it.*"

"*A hawk?*"

"Yes, those crows want to kill the hawk. Would you mind if I try to help the hawk? She couldn't know, yet, that I planned to throw things at the crows, that I would chant, clap and yell – do anything – to get the crows to leave the hawk alone.

I hate crows, she said. I smiled my agreement almost sardonically. She led me through the house and into her back yard. I walked to the tree, looked up, and could see immediately that I was correct. The crows *were* attacking the hawk, for no apparent reason.

I grabbed some pine cones from around the base of the tree and threw them at the crows. One, two, then ten, but the crows ignored me. My neighbor declared more than asked, "*What else can we do?*"

I saw a hose over to the side, so I said, *Water. Let's try water.* I stretched the hose from the house to the tree, while my neighbor turned on the spigot. I aimed the water at the crows perched on the lower branches. They scattered. I aimed higher. But the water would not squirt any higher. The crows continued to attack the hawk while the hawk remained stoic and impervious to their murderous intent.

By now, I realized that nothing was going to work. I drew in closer to the tree to get a better look. I squinted because the light of the afternoon sun was in my eyes. I thought – yes, I could see – the hawk was holding onto something, something black clutched in the hawk's talons. A crow. ...

A

baby ...

crow.

Things are seldom as they appear.

Sometimes, a story is just a story. Sometimes, a story is philosophy. Or theology. Or spiritual. Sometimes a story is all of the above. Regardless, the best stories are ironic.

Judges interpreting written law follow long-standing guidelines, called rules of interpretation. One of these rules, *legislative intent*, calls upon the judge to ask what the legislature intended when it originally passed the law. What were the legislators thinking? What public arguments did they make to support the law? What did they hope to accomplish by enacting the law?

Another such rule is the "plain-meaning" rule, applied when it is obvious from the face of the law what it means. No further interpretive inquiry is necessary, absent some clear and compelling reason.

Many of the stories about Jesus and the parables and aphorisms he told require no further interpretive inquiry. Their meaning is obvious from the text.

The meaning of other such stories and sayings are not so obvious, in which case further inquiry is warranted. Consider, for example, this aphorism: ...*if you do not forgive others, neither will your Father forgive your trespasses.* (Matt. 6:15) Your forgiveness is contingent upon your forgiving others. Plainly read. Yet, Jesus offered this aphorism to interpret that part of the Lord's Prayer, ... *forgive us our debts, as we also have forgiven our debtors.* (Matt. 6:12) Why did Jesus feel the need to interpret something that seems obvious on its face? (Partly, I would suggest, because people struggle so much with forgiving others.)

What is a trespass against you? Something that hurts your feelings? Or a violation of your personhood? Do you forgive others before they ask for your forgiveness, or do you wait until they acknowledge their breach? Does forgiveness require you to resist evil, or to stand passively by while evil is perpetrated upon you or someone else?

The concept of forgiving others is complex. Both the plain-meaning reading and further elucidation become important in practice, requiring wisdom above all else.

In fact, scholars apply any number of tools to interpret Scripture. Yes, they apply a plain meaning to Scripture, but they also attempt to place the writing in its context, both historically and literally. What was happening with the people at the time? What were their struggles, politically and personally? Scholars acknowledge linguistics, the difficulty, for example, of translating a Hebrew acrostic poem into English.[1]

Because of the difficulty, if not impossibility, of elucidating a single and precise meaning of Biblical myths, poems, prayers, sayings and stories, one must ask whether we were ever intended to reduce Scripture to the singular. Perhaps we Christians could learn from our rabbinical brethren, who often eschew answers in favor of questions. Questions can be liberating, liberating even the text, especially an obtuse or obscure text.

The story of Abraham's sacrifice of Isaac is an example of a story treated by rabbis as being subject to a variety of interpretations. Known as *Akedah,* the story might have to do with trust in God (*Abraham trusted God,* the writer to the Hebrews interprets, *and it was attributed to him as righteousness.*). But the *Akedah* might just as easily be a polemic against those sacrificing children, believed to have been a common practice of the day. What about the relationships behind the stories – how angry would Sarah have been at Abraham when Isaac came home to tell her, *Dad tried to kill me.*

---

[1] An acrostic poem is one in which the first letter of each line forms its own word. Because the Hebrew alphabet is different from most other alphabets, an acrostic poem originally written in Hebrew naturally loses its deeper meaning when translated.

Jesus was a rabbi, wasn't he? The religious leaders used the honorific, whether sarcastically or literally, who can know? But he *was* a teacher, familiar with and perhaps schooled in the tradition. His sayings and actions consist of multifaceted and layered meanings, much like the skin of an onion. Peel the onion, one layer at a time. Nuance and hidden meaning, Jesus inverted and reinterpreted Scripture. (*You have heard that it was said, "An eye for an eye and a tooth for a tooth." But I say to you, Do not resist an evildoer. But if anyone strikes you on the right cheek, turn the other also* ... Matt. 5:38-39)

I believe Jesus spoke the way we speak, seldom if ever intending each word or phrase to be taken literally. I like to tell jokes that should never be taken literally.[2] Sarcasm leaks into any conversation, as do metaphor and hyperbole. I do not speak allegorically very often, although Jesus seems to have done so.

Just how much of Jesus' speech was literal? If you believe that the Gospel according to Mark harbors a hidden "Messianic secret," then you must confess that a plain reading of that gospel would be incomplete at best, and misleading at worst. Jesus' stories, aphorisms, and parables are layered like mica with meaning upon meaning.

All of this is to say that Jesus could be ironic. He was a storyteller, and every good story has irony. I do not mean the pedestrian concept of irony as something funny, haha. Rather, irony is the surprise, the unexpected conclusion to an anticipated series of events. The paschal mystery, the death, burial and resurrection of Jesus, is itself ironic. Perhaps that same mystery is shrouded in further irony, for

---

[2] Like the one about the priest, preacher and rabbi asked to consecrate a Ferrari. The priest blessed the car with holy water, while the preacher prayed over it in the name of Jesus. The rabbi cut two inches off the tailpipe. Or the one in which the man walking through the department store came to the escalator, and he decided to go up to the next floor. Only there was a sign next to the escalator that read, *You must carry your dog*. Taking the sign literally, the man thought to himself, *where am I going to find a dog?*

what appears to be physical, the resurrection of Jesus, is at least in some respects spiritual or super-physical – hence, the translation of Jesus' body through walls into a closed room.

The writers themselves – Matthew, Mark, Luke and John – placed their Jesus stories in a sequence that would support their theses, not chronologically according to the sequence of events. Hence, John writes as though Jesus' ministry spanned three Passover celebrations in Jerusalem, whereas the others tell about one Passover spent in Jerusalem, reducing Jesus' ministry to just one year. Was Jesus' public ministry three years long, or just one?

Mark's story appears at first to be a straight-line story of the public life of Jesus. Many scholars now see a *Messianic Secret* tucked deep within the story. Mark writes his thesis early in the story: *Who then is this, that even the wind and the sea obey him?*, (Mark 4:41), and answers it at the end, when a Roman centurion reflects on Jesus at his death, *Truly this was God's Son!"* (Mark 15:39)

John's story is anything but straight-line. The Last Supper as the institution of the Eucharist is not described at all, but instead there is this foot-washing that John presents as an interpretation of the Eucharist. Service is holy. Things are not what they appear to be, and the Eucharist, writes John, is not about mere elements of bread and wine. John thus reduces the question of whether the bread becomes the literal body of Christ to something nonsensical and comical.

Irony might include humor, but it might not. Humor is not a prerequisite to irony, whereas *surprise* is. The hawk is the culprit, not the crows. Things are not as they appear.

I wrote this little book to consider alternative paths into the stories presented. Although I suggest re-interpretation, the purpose of this book is to engage you, not just intellectually, but in your faith. Faith and grace, and Jesus was about so much more than straight-line living and teaching.

Indeed, I cannot help but imagine Jesus had fun with his congregation – perhaps he was playful even. If so, then shouldn't we be equally playful with the exquisite stories and sayings of his that we have as our guide? What is holy about Scripture, anyway, if not its ability to open wide the portal for you to enter God's companion universe?

My hope, of course, is that you will take other Jesus stories and find new light in them. Enjoy and rejoice!

Chapter 1

Faith and Leaning into God (or God's Leaning into You)

While [Jesus] was still speaking to the crowds, his mother and his brothers were standing outside, wanting to speak to him. Someone told him, "Look, your mother and your brothers are standing outside, wanting to speak to you." But to the one who had told him this, Jesus replied, "Who is my mother, and who are my brothers?" And pointing to his disciples, he said, "Here are my mother and my brothers! For whoever does the will of my Father in heaven is my brother and sister and mother."

That same day Jesus went out of the house and sat beside the sea. Such great crowds gathered around him that he got into a boat and sat there, while the whole crowd stood on the beach. And he told them many things in parables, saying: "Listen! A sower went out to sow. And as he sowed, some seeds fell on the path, and the birds came and ate them up. Other seeds fell on rocky ground, where they did not have much soil, and they sprang up quickly, since they had no depth of soil. But when the sun rose, they were scorched; and since they had no root, they withered away. Other seeds fell among thorns, and the thorns grew up and choked them. Other seeds fell on good soil and brought forth grain, some a hundredfold, some sixty, some thirty. Let anyone with ears listen!"

Then the disciples came and asked him, "Why do you speak to them in parables?" He answered, "To you it has been given to know the secrets of the kingdom of heaven, but to them it has not been given. For to those who have, more will be given, and they will have an abundance; but from those who have nothing, even what they have will be taken away. The reason I speak to them in parables is that 'seeing they do not perceive, and hearing they do not listen, nor do they understand.' With them indeed is fulfilled the prophecy of Isaiah that says:

'You will indeed listen, but never understand,
   and you will indeed look, but never perceive.

> For this people's heart has grown dull,
>> and their ears are hard of hearing,
>>> and they have shut their eyes;
>>>> so that they might not look with their eyes,
>>> and listen with their ears,
>> and understand with their heart and turn—
>>> and I would heal them.'

But blessed are your eyes, for they see, and your ears, for they hear. Truly I tell you, many prophets and righteous people longed to see what you see, but did not see it, and to hear what you hear, but did not hear it. (Matthew 12:46-13:17)

A man approached the mall escalator. He noticed a sign posted next to it: *Dogs must be carried on escalator.*

The man looked about anxiously and asked, *Where in the world am I going to find a dog?*

I, like most people, would like clear answers to baffling questions, a map to guide me through life's maze of choices. Should I take the new job? Should I move across the country? Should I try yet again to reconcile with that friend who stopped talking to me years ago? Should I reach out to the person who may not want my help?

I need guidance. My questions are honest and sincere. I desire to do the "right thing," even when I do not know what that "right thing" may be. Why don't I know? Why is God often silent?

Life can feel like a looking-glass world, only I remind myself that the Apostle Paul described feeling the same way. He detested some of his own actions, but couldn't quite bring himself to do better. Trapped perversely in some cosmic battle of sin over soul or soul over sin, Paul asked the most relevant question: where is God?

Of course my struggle is far more pedestrian than Paul's. Paul's was a moral struggle between right and wrong; mine is a mortal struggle to find meaning. I just want to follow the path to a life well-lived. Will my life prove to be meaningful, or will I spend it nihilistically on a treadmill like a rat running nowhere?

I want a sign, but the only sign Jesus seems to be offering is the one offered to his own "evil" generation: *the sign of the prophet*. *For just as Jonah was three days and three nights in the belly of the sea monster ...* . (*See* Matt. 12:38-41)

Dogs must be carried, only I do not have a dog to carry. The sign of Jonah and three days seems nonsensical.

Jesus *openly* hid truths from well-meaning people. He spoke in occlusive parables, that they might see and not perceive, hear and not understand. *Why not perceive, and why not understand?*

Dogs must be carried, but why not post instead, *Dogs are not allowed on the escalator unless they are carried*? If you want somebody to understand your meaning, state the instruction plainly.

I concur with the disciples' querulous tone when they asked Jesus, *Why do you speak to them in parables?*

Jesus' answer is baffling:

> *To you it has been given to know the secrets of the kingdom of heaven, but to them it has not been given. For to those who have, more will be given, and they will have an abundance; but from those who have nothing, even what they have will be taken away. The reason I speak to them in parables is that 'seeing they do not perceive, and hearing they do not listen, nor do they understand.* (Matt. 13:11-13)

Jesus added words from the prophet Isaiah: *so that they might not look with their eyes, and listen with their ears, and understand with their heart and turn – and I would heal them.* (Matt. 13:15; *cf.* Isaiah 6:9)

Wait a minute. Did Jesus not *come to seek out and to save the lost*? (Lk. 19:10). Are not the religious leaders – the Pharisees, Sadducees, lawyers – those most lost of all?

Had Jesus sincerely desired to save those most lost, he might have simplified faith to the point where even we religious leaders (myself included) might see and hear with heart and soul and perceive and be saved? Jesus saves, but not everybody. Please speak plainly,

Jesus, so we all might understand! *Hidden from the foundation of the world,* Matthew describes Jesus' truths. (Matt.13:34, 35)

Hidden, yet when spoken, nonetheless mysterious. Like the diamond hidden from the foundation, only just now pulled from the earth – it is dirty and looks like common quartz – but oh, the treasure!

Unlocking parables? Finding diamonds and hidden truths? How?

Jesus gave Peter keys to unlock the kingdom. (Matt. 16:19) The Roman Catholics take Jesus literally, meaning that Jesus conferred upon Peter and his successors as popes the authority to unlock heaven's gate to those eligible for entry. Popes carry these keys around in their pockets, forgiving or retaining sins, communing or excommunicating people.

Protestants, on the other hand, believe the keys are not found on a person, but in correct teaching. When Jesus gave Peter the keys, Peter had just proclaimed Jesus as Messiah. This truth, Jesus as Messiah, is the foundational teaching upon which the church is built, the keys to unlock the door.

In my estimation, both Roman Catholics and Protestants have it wrong. The *Petrine* keys are not authoritarian, not from an hierarchical standpoint or a doctrinal standpoint. Instead, Peter's keys unlock relationship.

Juxtapose Peter against the religious leaders. The religious leaders of Jesus' day imagined that relationship with God was about doing the right thing, worshipping the correct way, living a moral life, or belonging to or being born into the right tribe. The problem with their approach is what I noted at the outset: life can appear *ambiguous,* and *doing right* frequently means choosing not between good and bad, but between good and good. Life can feel like walking through thick fog.

And in the end, the indicia of a good life is the approach one takes, not the results one achieves. Journey over destination. Who you become is more important than what you do. Peter was a follower. He followed a person. The religious leaders followed law. One had heart; the others did not.

Matthew

When Matthew stitched the quilt of his Gospel, he did so from bit pieces of other cloths. He plagiarized Mark, often word for word. He and Luke borrowed from the "Q" source as well, and each had at least one other unidentified, independent source. Of course Matthew attempted to be faithful to the actual story, but he told the story in a way that would help him accomplish his goals. What were his goals?

Matthew wanted to strengthen and encourage the new community ("church") formed around the resurrection event. Matthew is the only Gospel writer who actually used the word, "church" ("ecclesia"), and he used it twice.[3] He used *ecclesia* because the new community was struggling with its identity. It was comprised primarily of Jewish Christians, Jews who chose to live out their Judaism through Christ. (The original *Jews for Jesus*, if you will.) These Jewish men and women understood their faith as coalescing around the central event of Jesus as the Christ – lived through his teaching, crucifixion and resurrection. They experienced acute opposition from Jewish religious leaders who seemed to be more interested in a superficial obedience to law than in exercising actual faith.

In the face of such opposition, Matthew's new Christian community needed answers to a set of fundamental questions: did Messiah Jesus have to die? Why did he have to die? Why did he have to die at the hands of their own people – the Jewish leaders – rather than at the hands of the Roman occupiers? Matthew tried to

---

[3] Use of "ecclesia" in Matthew is an anachronism, a concept developed following the resurrection and inserted into the Gospel by Matthew as though Jesus understood its post-resurrection meaning.

address these critical questions by organizing Jesus' teaching and life into his Gospel.

Hence, Matthew's Jesus spoke of a kingdom whose king is God, rather than of Israel and the limited group of people called Israelites. Matthew repeatedly presented stories in terms of kingdom, and often these stories included a king, who was God.

Consider the Lord's Prayer. It is nothing, if not a *kingdom* prayer. *[Y]our kingdom come ... on earth as in heaven,* (Matt. 6:10, Jer.). God as father is king, and the three main petitions, for food, forgiveness, and for evil to be kept at bay, are all markers of God's kingdom. Plentiful food, plentiful forgiveness, an absence of evil.

Matthew, however, was particularly *Jewish,* in that he affirmed the Jewishness of his Jewish Christian church. He told the story of Messiah, not just as Son of Man/Son of God, but also as Isaiah's suffering servant. (*cf.* Matt. 26:63-65) The church became the natural inheritor of the promises of Abraham, not because of blood, but of faith. (*See* Matt. 3:9, John the Baptist calling upon people to look beyond their Jewish heritage as the fundamental marker of faith.)

As a primarily Jewish story, Moses plays a dominant, though invisible, role. In fact, Matthew's Jesus is a new Moses. Consider that both Jesus and Moses were exiled Hebrew babies in Egypt. Both babies threatened leaders in such a way that these leaders murdered all of the baby boys of their generation, yet both Moses and Jesus were miraculously saved. Both Jesus' and Moses' ministries were preceded by wilderness experiences of disturbed selves.

Moses issued a new law from Mount Sinai, and Jesus interpreted Moses' law while teaching people from the side of a mountain. (*See* Matt. 5:1, *"Sermon on the Mount"*)

I say not to you an eye for an eye and a tooth for a tooth .... but if your brother asks you to go one mile with him, go two. ... I came not to abolish the law and the prophets, but to fulfill them. (*See generally,* Matt. 5-7, *paraphrased*) By healing on the Sabbath, Jesus reinterpreted the commandment regarding Sabbath rest.

As a new Moses, Jesus distinguished between those people who were part of the new community of faith from those who were not. Peter's gate to the new community called upon people to walk through a *spiritual* understanding of the law rather than a literal one, and a spiritual understanding of Jesus' life (and resurrection).

Matthew and Jesus' Relations

Jesus' family was standing *outside*. (*See* Matt. 12:46-50) They had come to speak to Jesus. Jesus disputed their relationship, and pointed instead to those inside: *these* are my mother and my brothers—these disciples, who do the will of the Father. These members of the new community are my family.

Jesus was not rejecting or condemning his mother and brothers; he was using metaphor and hyperbole to elevate the connection people experience by relationship in Matthew's new community, the *ecclesia*. Relationship by spirit is a closer connection among people than that by blood. Relationship by spirit to God is tighter than that by blood.

The parable of the sower follows immediately. Matthew placed the parable of the sower in this location intentionally, as though saying, my brothers and mother and sisters are those whose hearts are fertile, loamy soil receptive of grace.

Grace, Faith, Good Works and Right Thinking

Most people tend to shun grace. Grace is hard, trusting completely in something beyond oneself. The illusion of good works or right thinking is far easier, relying on oneself and one's own abilities. Reliance on self is the magnetic opposite of grace, and has the effect of repelling grace.

Think here of the person who treats the Nicene Creed as *shibboleth*, who believes someone is not Christian unless she mentally agrees with the Creed in toto. Yet, it is not the words that count; it is the posture of the soul that counts. Struggling with the *virginity of Mary*, or the physicality of the resurrection, strengthens faith, rather than diminishes it; struggle is a pitchfork that turns the soil of the heart, creating rich soil out of rock and clay. The Latin word, *Credo* – I believe – does not mean, *I think*. It means something along the lines of *I give myself to*. I donate myself to. I belong to God the Father Almighty.

Many people defend their unwillingness to believe in Christianity's God by pointing to hypocritical Christians. *I can't believe because Christians are a bunch of hypocrites. They talk the talk but don't walk the walk*. Indeed, but faith was never about perfect behavior. It will always be about struggle – Paul's and mine – sin's and life. *All have sinned and fallen short*. And, another person's failure is never an excuse for my own failure – to try. Seed among thorns.

What about the hardened heart, the person whose life experiences have been so painful, or hurtful, that seed cannot find its purchase in their souls? Birds of the air snatch the seed away. Rocky soil, too, and the roots find no depth.[4]

Jesus' parables are not all fun and games, but address the hard parts of life. Most of the seed cast by the sower fails to grow into a mature plant. Moreover, there is no escaping dualism in Jesus' parable(s). Some people appear to be intrinsically good to Jesus, while others appear to be intrinsically evil. The good are wheat gathered into the barn, and the evil are chaff burned by fire. Separated at the end of the age, and metaphor or not, the language wafts of burning rubber.

Only harsh language speaks to choice, not so much about hell and eternal damnation, but choice to live faith – take the journey – rather than eschew it. Struggle rather than hide. Wrestle with God and, like Jacob, pin God to the ground (and then walk with the limp of faith forever). But in the end, I have a say in my own

---

[4] Jesus' use of soils is metaphor, and it is easy – as I am doing in some ways – to reduce the metaphor to literal interpretation. There is no "one size fits all," and when it comes to faith, I myself have been soil that is rocky or a path or even rich and loamy.

destiny. I have free will. I can choose good over evil. Or path over wilderness.

Matthew's new community of believers are now the insiders, the new brothers, the new mother, the new sisters of Jesus. To them is given the key, the faith, the hope – but pay attention – this faith, this secret from the foundation of the world, is relational. It is foremost about family and how one views and treats God, not how good a person is or even how "accurately" the person thinks/believes.

Peter acknowledged Jesus as Messiah, and Jesus responded, *flesh and blood has not revealed this [secret] to you*, Peter. (Matt. 16:17) The secret is otherworldly. You, Peter, therefore receive the keys to the kingdom, binding and loosing. Welcoming and damning. Roman Catholics have long and incorrectly assumed the metaphoric keys made Peter the first pope. Their interpretation is nonsense.

Peter never thought of himself as pope, and Jesus' brother, James, (according to The Acts of the Apostles) was head of the early church, not Peter. Moreover, no pope was elected until the thirteenth century. Many of the so-called popes were declared to be so posthumously, while during their lives, they thought of themselves far more simply: Bishop of Rome, co-equal in authority and status to the Bishops of Jerusalem, Constantinople, Alexandria, and Antioch (these five having been the original five *sees* of the Church).

Many Protestant denominations teach that Jesus did not intend Peter to become pope holding keys. Rather, they say, the keys are the truth of Peter's declaration: Jesus is Messiah. (*You are the Messiah, the Son of the Living God,* Peter had said. (Matt. 16:16)) The danger in this understanding is that it tends to reduce faith to an intellectual exercise (by which one must *think* Jesus is Messiah). Thinking is advantageous when it comes to describing faith, but not when it comes to creating faith. One cannot think one's way into faith. One yields to God, and that becomes the *exercise* of faith. One follows, and that becomes faith. One trusts, and that becomes faith.

Hence, a person might have faith and yet wrestle with the concept of the divinity of Jesus. She might lean into Jesus for help (and would that not be faith?), but not appreciate fully who this person Jesus is. Even Paul did not appreciate fully who the person Jesus was at his conversion. He responded to the blinding light not because he understood, but because he was *confronted* by the force of Jesus.

And so, faith becomes the boat sailing through the choppy waters of uncertainty. It is about leaning into, donating oneself to, about belonging to. Not correct wording, nor superior personage.

Paul claims, and many Christians quote, that if you believe in your heart and confess with your mouth that Jesus is Lord, you will be saved. These Christians are "proof-texting," using a particular Scripture verse to uphold an approach that worked for them. They turn this approach into a universal requirement, even though it was particular to them and their experience. Not everybody comes to faith the same way.

Moreover, when Paul speaks of faith as saving, he is ambiguous about *whose* faith saves. Is it yours, or Jesus' faith? Your leaning into God, or God leaning into you?

If Jesus had wanted Christians to observe only *one* formula in order to locate salvation, however one might define "salvation,"[5] he would have told the rich young ruler, *believe in your heart and confess with your mouth that I am Lord*. Jesus offered this man not so much as a talisman, except to advise him to do what is truly hard: sell all you have and give the money to the poor. I wonder why more preachers don't tell people to sell all they have and give the money to the poor? To be saved *that way*? Wouldn't you expect

---

[5] The definition of salvation requires a separate discussion. Suffice it to say that Jesus typically did not refer to eternal salvation when speaking of salvation, and certainly not the way we tend to think of eternal salvation. Jesus was concerned about bringing the kingdom of God to earth as in heaven – suggesting salvation is about the here and now. Moreover, if one looks carefully, one can find echoes of universality in Jesus' teachings and the Gospels.

them to choose Jesus' formula for salvation over Paul's? But – and this is the point – neither is a formula for salvation. There is no formula.

James, much to the consternation of Martin Luther, wrote that good works are requisite to faith, and by extension, salvation. *Faith without works is dead* – it is a void, a red herring, a tail chasing. There's no there there, without good works. Yet, I can never be *good* enough.

And doesn't all of this render salvation a moving target? Relying upon Peter's confession of faith for one's salvation is tantamount to seed falling upon the trodden path. It is not Peter's confession of faith that is foundational, but his relationship to Jesus. It's about relationship. The keys in Peter's hand unlock relationship.

Peter is Jesus' brother, his mother, his sister. The truth of Peter's confession is not found in the words themselves, but in the posture Peter assumes with Jesus. Jesus is God's *messiah*, God's revelation to the world, the incarnation of God, and hidden deep within this sphere of truth, Peter found faith.

The irony of these parables about heaven and hell, about wheat and chaff, about those who are in and those who are out, is the irony of faith itself, that you can think you are in, but you aren't, and the minute you think you've made it, you've removed yourself from the IT.

…Then who can be saved?… For mortals it is impossible, but for God, all things are possible. (Matt. 19:25, 26)

Some people get it. Some people don't. Some people understand. Some do not. Even Peter, though understanding, understood only partway: Jesus as Messiah (*Son of the Living God!*), yes, but suffering servant, no. Some see, but do not perceive. Some see only in part. And Jesus rebuked Peter immediately after praising him: *Get thee behind me, Satan.* (KJV, Matt. 16:23) Pope one minute, Satan the next.

The Jewish religious establishment was blind, hardened by a perverse need to preserve the status quo or their power or whatever it was that was blocking their deeper spirituality. We've all known people who were sick yet refused a doctor's help. Change requires relinquishment.

The seed fell on all types of soil, but only one type of soil facilitates germination. Only one type of soil sustains a plant to maturity: loamy soil, rich, turned and aged, deep brown or black, welcoming.

Which means, in the end, I must sail through life as through the choppy waters of uncertainty. Direction, guidance, salvation and even hope are there, but blindly. The signs will always be ambiguous, otherwise I would be tempted not to rely upon God, but upon the signs. Upon formula. Upon myself. Faith means reliance upon personhood, which makes it about relationship, and relationship alone. Imagine that – relationship to the Living God!

Chapter 2

Walking on Water is Not Faith

Immediately he made the disciples get into the boat and go on ahead to the other side, while he dismissed the crowds. And after he had dismissed the crowds, he went up the mountain by himself to pray. When evening came, he was there alone, but by this time the boat, battered by the waves, was far from the land, for the wind was against them. And early in the morning he came walking toward them on the sea. But when the disciples saw him walking on the sea, they were terrified, saying, "It is a ghost!" And they cried out in fear. But immediately Jesus spoke to them and said, "Take heart, it is I; do not be afraid."
Peter answered him, "Lord, if it is you, command me to come to you on the water." He said, "Come." So Peter got out of the boat, started walking on the water, and came toward Jesus. But when he noticed the strong wind, he became frightened, and beginning to sink, he cried out, "Lord, save me!" Jesus immediately reached out his hand and caught him, saying to him, "You of little faith, why did you doubt?" When they got into the boat, the wind ceased. And those in the boat worshiped him, saying, "Truly you are the Son of God." Matt. 14:22-33 (*cf. Mark 6:45-52, John 6:16-21*)

Jesus *constrained*[6] the disciples to get into the boat and go to the other side (Mark 6:45), leaving him alone for the second time in as many chapters. Jesus had just received the dark news that his cousin, John, had been beheaded at Herod's hand, news Jesus needed to process with prayer. (Matthew 14:13) He tried to steal away from the crowd, but they followed him anyway. He fed them. After they ate, Jesus tried to be alone again and sent both the crowd

---

[6] KJV, Matthew and Mark.

and his disciples away, the crowd by land and his disciples by boat. (*See* Mark)

Conflating the Gospels and relying upon tradition, it appears as though Jesus and John grew up together as cousins.[7] Perhaps John was Jesus' only *real* friend. Both became preachers, their symbiotic lives entangled and wrapped into and about each other like strands of rope. The only way each existed and accomplished his work was with and because of the other. If anybody understood Jesus, it must have been John, and if anybody understood John, it must have been Jesus. John preached, *Prepare the way,* and Jesus *was* the Way. John preached, *Turn from your sins,* and Jesus *became* sin as a mechanism to remove the human blight from the world.[8] Jesus and John lived co-dependent lives and expressed co-dependent ministries, sharing mutually dependent pasts and mutually dependent destinies.

Sometimes Jesus sounded egocentric in his preaching. *I am the way, the truth, and the life.* (John 14:6) *For where two or three are gathered together in my name ...* (Matt. 18:20) *... see, something greater than Solomon is here.* (Matt. 12:42) Yet his *way* or *path* was not solo; it required John's advance work.

Repent, John preached to prepare the people for Jesus. *Who warned you to flee from the wrath to come?* he demanded of both the religious leaders, (Matt. 3:7), and the people (Luke 3:7). John's invective was both corporate and personal, delivered to the nation as a whole, and to people individually. John kneaded the chewy dough of the human soul to soften it, to tenderize the calloused hearts of a people belonging to God. Sweep the floor, dust the furniture, and make the house ready for the guest to be sent by God.

---

[7] The Gospel According to John is ambiguous about Jesus and John's early relationship.

[8] I choose not to wade into any discussion about atonement theology, instead taking Paul's statement at face value: *he who knew no sin became sin on our behalf ...* (2 Cor. 5:21) On a personal note, I prefer to think of sin as darkness or evil, something that Jesus submitted to in order to overcome.

John's ministry became Act One in a three-act play,[9] and now both friend and cousin of Jesus was dead – murdered. Imagine the acute grief Jesus felt when he heard of John's fate; imagine his agonizing need to be alone.

Jesus left Galilee by boat to a desert place, also called *lonely*. (Matt. 14:13, Jer.)

This was not the first time Jesus sequestered himself. Following his baptism, Jesus fled to the lonely wilderness to battle demons for forty days. In the wilderness, a person can believe he is the only person still alive. You, plus God. No crowds nor parties, no tugging on the cloak nor demands on your time, and no expectations to behave in a socially acceptable manner.

Old *Celtic* thin places, where the space between this dimension and the next one is infinitesimal. You wrestle devils and God in lonely places. You confuse God for the devil in lonely places.[10] When destitute of soul and hope, you prostrate yourself in a *lonely* place, lay prone before God and the universe by body and soul. God rescues you in *that* wilderness, in *that* destitution, in *that* desolation.

Jesus needed to be alone because, as only the co-dependent can appreciate, the loss of the other is a loss of self. Everything changes when the *other* is gone.

That first time Jesus left, the crowds became scandalized. They needed Jesus. Where had he gone? Would he return, and if so, when? The crowd became like the disciples who, when torrential seas rocked their boat, shook Jesus awake and accused him: *Teacher, do you not care that we are perishing?* (Mark 4:38)

These predictable people snaked their long lines of lonely hearts along wilderness paths of hillside grass to find Jesus. Dozens at first, then hundreds, and finally thousands of them looking for Jesus and

---

[9] The third act belongs to the Holy Spirit and the church.
[10] Recall the Genesis story of Jacob wrestling with and pinning God, refusing to let God go until God promised to bless Jacob. (*See* Gen. 32:22-31)

God's assurance that they were not nihilistically alone, for some hint that God really *does* care, and not just that *we're going to die?*

I imagine Jesus perched on a rock overlooking the sea, watching people zigzag their crooked ways toward him. Was it a vision, or was this real? Hungry souls, but why are these people seeking sustenance in a countryside where there is no food?

Alternatively, I imagine Jesus standing in the boat anchored to shore. People are gathering at the water's edge, cutting down from the hillside above, waving hands. *We're here! Jesus, we found you! You must have lost us, but we found you.*

Jesus waives back. *I see you. I see you,* he answers. I see you, and I see your lonely hearts. Jesus becomes aroused and moved with compassion. He heals their sick and feeds their empty stomachs.

But this means Jesus still needs to be alone, yet cannot find a way to *that* place. On that fatal day he learned of John's death. Even after hearing the news, he fed the 5,000 men, plus women and children. He took the bread, looked up to heaven, blessed and broke it, and watched the disciples distribute it to the people.

Nobody fed Jesus. His cousin, friend and counterpart was dead. He was bereft and prepared to go to sleep that night alone and empty, perhaps even hungry. *My food is to do the will of him who sent me,* Jesus' disciples once overheard him say, (John 4:34), and *one does not live by bread alone ....* (See Mt. 4:4)

Once the people had eaten, Jesus dismissed them and *constrained* the disciples to go to the other side. *Go before me to the other side,* he instructed. Time for Jesus to be alone. At last.

Now, should you ask me which of Jesus' miracles I might like to see performed, or better yet, to perform, it would be walking on water. I tried it once, but sank.

I was a teenager who had already had an experience of faith and believed in the importance of prayer. I tell you this only so you will understand who I was at the time the following stories took place, and why I prayed when Kim lost her contact lens.

My father ran The Reef Motel, a small resort in Vero Beach, Florida. We spent summers at the Reef, body surfing and snorkeling in the ocean, walking the beach, and playing Marco Polo in the swimming pool. Our *Crayola* white backsides were perpetually sunburnt, and we made friends with kids from Ohio and New Hampshire and Chicago. Those summer days were blissful and lazy.

Sometimes I would wander off by myself, walk the beach, build a castle, or swim in the pool. In the pool by myself, I'd dive deep, hang near the bottom, then push my toes against the bottom to surface and breathe, much like a whale will surface, breathe, then fall back to the cooler water below. Up and down, breathing only when I had to, letting myself feel the water hold me, exquisitely lonely and innately spiritual (which I did not appreciate as such for another forty years).

I also learned to "do" flips and inwards off the diving board during those summers. I became a good diver and joined my high school diving team. We were a rag-tag B-team that always lost to the A-teams, but we had fun.

I learned that to spring-dive effectively, the diver must dive deep to the bottom of the twelve-foot competition swimming pool. As a corollary, I learned *not* to dive deep in my father's eight-foot vacation pool. When I would spring off of that board, I would hold my hands stiffly out in front of me to prevent myself from banging my head on the bottom. One rainy day, I was swimming alone in the pool and forgot to hold my hands out.

Swim Rule No. 1: Never swim alone. Yes, I was a good swimmer who stupidly assumed the risk. Daydreaming, I started bouncing on the diving board, low at first, then higher and higher like I was jumping on a trampoline. I looked out at the ocean beyond the pool and yard. The sky was gunmetal grey.

As I bounced on the board, I thought about school and friends, of our upcoming junior year, plus all the other things that teenagers daydream about. I recalled the summer just past, and one of my new friends, Mark, from Chicago, and the two girls we had met. Angst, too, my teenage mind gilded with angst, lodged deep in thought as I bounced. Almost by habit, as I continued to jump higher and higher, I finally dove. Without a thought, a straight and simple dive, instinctual and deep. My head slammed into the concrete bottom of the pool. I saw stars and almost blacked out. I might have drowned, only I didn't black out and I didn't drown. And I do not know to this day whether my survival was a miracle, simple grace, or that I wasn't as alone at the pool as I had imagined myself to be.

I witnessed one other strange event at that swimming pool. I was swimming with my friend Kim, who was also on the swim team. She and I had grown close riding to swim meets on the bus together. We'd listen to the radio play the same songs over and over again: *We've got to get right back where we started from ...* [11]

Also a gray day when nobody else was at the pool, Kim and I were chatting it up and swimming. Kim wore contact lenses, which in those days were both permanent and expensive.

Swimming Rule No. 2: Take your contact lenses out of your eyes before swimming in a pool. When Kim opened her eyes underwater, one of the contact lenses popped out. Kim sprung out of the water like a porpoise and shouted, *I lost my contact!*

I was fairly pedestrian in those days, and Kim was eccentric. She liked to shock people, especially me, to liven things up. To this day we are good friends, and the dynamic has changed little. Anyway, when Kim shouted that she'd lost her contact, I looked at her sideways, and then with condescending pity. (*What were you thinking, swimming with your contacts in?*)

Typically I would not pray to find a lost contact lens. I did not and do not use my mustard-seed faith to manipulate mountains. But for some reason, I said, *let's ask for help.* And I promise you, this is true. Immediately following a quick prayer, I found Kim's contact lens using a mask and snorkel. Seventy-five thousand gallons of clear water and we found a clear contact lens in under three minutes.

---

[11] Pierre Tubbs and J. Vincent Edwards.

Let me say that again. I found Kim's clear contact lens floating in clear water on a cloudy day. I have no idea how this could be possible, save by some queer combination of prayer and innocence.

Yes, and those were days of immature faith and gi-normous hope and teenage angst and antics. And the miracle I *really* wanted to experience had nothing to do with the recovery of someone else's contact lenses in a swimming pool, but walking on water. Myself. I wanted to walk on water. Unfortunately, we do not get to choose our miracles.

There was no Harry Potter to read in those days, so I read about Jesus' miracles instead. Jesus walked through walls. He created food out of nothing. He levitated. He walked on water. And every time I read about this trick of Jesus', I would think to myself, *That's what I want to do, walk on water.* I suppose I wanted to rise above my own humanity, my own mediocrity.

People followed Jesus into the wilderness because they, too, wanted to rise above mediocrity. They were *sore* afraid. People always seem to be *afraid*. Afraid Jesus would leave them behind; afraid because they were sick and knew this man Jesus could heal them; afraid because the Romans were occupying their hometowns around Galilee; afraid that God had abandoned them to the Romans, or worse yet, to themselves. People are *sore* afraid.

One day, when nobody was watching, I tried walking on water. I stood at the edge of the pool full of children playing and surrounded by sunbathers. I stepped discretely from the side of the pool onto the concrete ledge surrounding the inside of the pool. Then I stepped further out, onto the even surface of the water. I saw the water as pavement.

In fact, God helped us find the contact lens, or so it seems. Also, I had experienced the internal shift of immoveable mountains by a faith that was not my own and came from someplace outside of myself. I *knew* by now that God could hold me on the top of that water, if she might. The problem was, I wasn't desperate. I wasn't hungry or sick. I didn't *need* to walk on water. I was, at best, whimsical, and at worst, egocentric.

Whimsical. Is God ever whimsical? God created *that Leviathan,* the Psalmist wrote, *just to amuse you.* (Ps. 104:26, Jer.) Whimsy, and this is the same God who walks through the garden during the cool of the day, who befriends the wanderer Abraham, who becomes irritated with irritating people. Jesus drank and ate with the wrong people – maybe because they needed help, or maybe because they were more fun. *Maybe* Jesus called Peter to follow him because Peter was the life of the party. Lampshade on head. Maybe there is more to Jesus and his disciples than appears. Could they be three-dimensional, and not just two-dimensional cardboard cutouts? Props?

I want to walk on water, too, Peter begged. Only, Jesus had *constrained* Peter and all the disciples to get into the boat and head to the other side.

Halfway across the Sea of Galilee, the tempest arises. The boat rocks; water sprays and sloshes across the bow. The dark sky and dim light of dusk occludes vision. The men cannot recall which is the correct direction in which to sail. Which side *is* the other side? All they can see is the bow of the boat, and barely that. Squinting through the hoary mist to locate the shore, they see a ghost walking towards them. Walking. Walking. Near to the boat. Passing. A bare filament, *mysterium tremendum,* only the form of the ghost *feels* vaguely familiar. *Déjà vu?* Jesus? But no, they left Jesus on shore. He instructed plainly, meet me on the other side, but how did he plan to get to the other side?[12] How does anybody make it to an opposite shore when so clearly stuck on the last one? If not by walking on water?

Jesus. He sees their distress, but now he is beyond them. In so many ways. Caustic wind and spray spits epithets at the disciples. These seasoned fishermen are *sore* afraid. You might ask, *What is a little squall to these fishermen?* Yet, they are *sore* afraid; so many people are *sore* afraid.

---

12 Why did the chicken cross the playground? To get to the other slide.

Wind and water is waging war against these soldiers of doubt. The ghost is a ghost, a figment – and haven't they seen Neptune anyway, rising out of the water at the end of long and fruitless fishing days? Neptune, reclaiming his own, and now the disciples cry out in raw desperation and primal fear.

Jesus cries out as well. *Stop it,* he orders. *Be not afraid; it is I!*

Time alone keeps them afloat, just minutes, now. Peter thinks it is Jesus. Hopes it is him. Doubts it is him. *If it is you, then beckon me come.* I want to walk on water, too. Or, I don't believe you. Or, I kind of believe – enough to get out of the boat – but not enough to feel the water as pavement.

Come, Jesus answers. Come if you must. Come if you doubt. Come if you still fear. Drop your nets, and come follow me. Come unto me all you that travail and are heavy laden and I will give you rest. For my burden is easy and my yoke is light. Take up your cross and come, follow me. *Come.*

Peter jumps recklessly out of the boat. The water is rock hard ground, like Petra himself. Peter trusts himself, relies upon himself. I believe. I can do it. This same self-ness that floated Peter as though he were on ground pulls him under as anchor. The water is rock and the rock is *w-a-t-e-r.* He is afraid. He cries out to Jesus or the disciples or anybody within earshot: *Save me!*

(Jesus once asked the disciples, *Are you going to leave me, like the others have left?* To which Peter replied, *Where would we go? You have the word of life.* (John 6:67-68, *para*) What *is* the word of life? Had Peter digested that word of life? Had I, as I stood at the edge of the swimming pool, been ready to step onto consumptive water? Who has a clue? Is faith about surety, or is it about hope? Faith and hope build their house together using lean-to desperation.)

Faith. The substance of things hoped for, the evidence of things not seen. There was no evidence the water was solid, so Peter sank.

They say, faith is not faith unless sandwiched between doubts. Or, two sides to one coin, faith is heads, and doubt is tails. But faith as substance must be pavement solid, supporting a very physical Jesus in the middle of the retributive sea.

Doesn't *faith come from hearing, and hearing by the Word of Christ?* (Rom. 10:17, *NASB*) Hadn't Jesus referred to himself as bread? Had Peter not eaten of this bread? (*See* John 6:68; *cf.* John 6:35; *cf., also,* Jeremiah 15:16.)

If faith and doubt aren't two sides to the same coin, two strands to the same rope, if the metaphors are inadequate, they are *just* inadequate, *just* incomplete. Doubt sharpens faith, and both are alchemy of heart and head, as in *I believe in God the Father Almighty.* My head believes, but what of my heart? Mere mental assent to the creeds is a shadow of faith, not faith itself. Religious dogma is at best dogma, experience put to words. Experience is primary; dogma is secondary. The only relevant questions are, *Who are you, O God, and Who am I?*

The word, *credo,* does not mean merely, *I believe,* as in mental assent. Its meaning is soul-deep, as in, *I give myself to* God, *father, son and spirit.* As in, I once stood over there, but now I stand rock-hard here, on this water that as liquid cannot possibly support me. Yet, my posture has changed, my geographic location. Once I was inside the boat and now I am outside the boat. *I believe, help my unbelief.* (Mk. 9:24) I am planted here, I am yours. Here I shall stay. I give myself to you.

Peter believes and doubts at once. On the one hand, Peter *believes* it is Jesus (*If it is you, tell me to come* ... the one word that compels faith, *come*). On the other hand, he disobeys Jesus' initial word of instruction. *Take the boat to the other side.* Peter becomes testy at Jesus' instruction, particularly in the face of waters raging. He wants more out of life than the beckoning call of the other side.

Peter wants to walk on water, so Jesus lets him. When Jesus tells Peter, *Come,* it is not because Jesus thinks that, with enough gumption, Peter can walk on water like Jesus. Jesus tells Peter, *Come,* because Jesus knows that Peter wants what Peter wants. So you see, Peter steps out of the boat not onto Jesus' word, but onto his own. There is no rock, no pavement, no *Petra* upon which Peter can stand; only water, so he sinks.

Faith comes by hearing and hearing by the Word of God. Jesus' word was, *Take the boat to the other side*, not, *walk on water*. But rather than take Peter to task for wanting to walk on water, Jesus taught Peter the faith lesson. *Come.* One whimsical word, *Come.* As in, *Let's see you try it.* As in, *Go ahead, Rob, step off the concrete ledge of the pool and see whether or not you will defy gravity and the principles of physics.* Whimsical Jesus must have been chuckling under his breath watching Peter step out of the boat. *There is that Leviathan that the Lord made to frolic.* The Lord never told Peter *not* to try it, nor did he chide me for stepping off the ledge of the pool and *onto* the water. Neither Peter nor I had faith. There can be no faith without the invitational Word from God. The mission, the strategy and purpose of God. Instead, each of us responded out of some primal fear, in my case egocentric anxiety – I was a teenager at the center of my own universe, faith notwithstanding – in the fisherman Peter's case, the churning waves and sea, faith notwithstanding.

No, Jesus did not chide Peter for trying. He chided Peter for losing sight of mission, which was to get to the other side. The Word had spoken: *Take the boat to the other side.* Faith provided the way there, despite the roiling sea. These men lost vision of mission for the obstructive churning of waves.

Who then is this, that even the wind and sea obey him? (Mk. 4:41) Why were the disciples so afraid? The Word they held deep in their hearts had slipped through cracks in their faith. *Step on a crack, you break your mother's back.* Jesus really *was* passing them by and frankly I doubt whether he cared at all that they saw him. He wasn't worried for them. *What, me worry?* Why should Jesus worry? He knew faith would carry them safely to the other side, if not their faith, then his.

How many times have I sunk in water because I could see surf and gale only, having lost sight of the other side?

In my life, I can count on both hands the few times I have been certain enough to know by grace that I had water as concrete to support me. On the other hand, I cannot count the number of times I've been pointed in a better direction. *Go to the other side.*

To get to the other side when all I have been able to see is water and waves and an occluded shoreline (if at all), God has forced me to rely upon the grace of relationship (with God). For this God whom even the wind and seas obey, well, this is the God who has brought me safe thus far, and this is the God who will lead me safely home.

Chapter 3

From each according to her abilities, to each according to her needs (The Marxism of Jesus)

"For the kingdom of heaven is like a landowner who went out early in the morning to hire laborers for his vineyard. After agreeing with the laborers for the usual daily wage, he sent them into his vineyard. When he went out about nine o'clock, he saw others standing idle in the marketplace; and he said to them, 'You also go into the vineyard, and I will pay you whatever is right.' So they went. When he went out again about noon and about three o'clock, he did the same. And about five o'clock he went out and found others standing around; and he said to them, 'Why are you standing here idle all day?' They said to him, 'Because no one has hired us.' He said to them, 'You also go into the vineyard.' When evening came, the owner of the vineyard said to his manager, 'Call the laborers and give them their pay, beginning with the last and then going to the first.' When those hired about five o'clock came, each of them received the usual daily wage. Now when the first came, they thought they would receive more; but each of them also received the usual daily wage. And when they received it, they grumbled against the landowner, saying, 'These last worked only one hour, and you have made them equal to us who have borne the burden of the day and the scorching heat.' But he replied to one of them, 'Friend, I am doing you no wrong; did you not agree with me for the usual daily wage? Take what belongs to you and go; I choose to give to this last the same as I give to you. Am I not allowed to do what I choose with what belongs to me? Or are you envious because I am generous?' So the last will be first, and the first will be last." Matt. 20:1-16 *(See generally, Matthew 19-20)*

Is heaven a geographic place? Is there an address on an e-map of the universe where you can pinpoint its location? Will GPS take you to heaven?

In Biblical times, people thought of heaven as a physical place. It occupied the sphere above the chasm that we call earth's atmosphere. The issue of the roundness of the earth was irrelevant to heaven's location, and Scripture hints at an earth both flat and spherical. What mattered to the people was the relative locations of (a) earth, (b) the biosphere containing the earth, and (c) the heaven that could be identified above or beyond the biosphere.

Sun, moon and stars were located within the biosphere. God and *the company of heaven,* which would have included all sorts of angels and cherubim and seraphim, were identified as existing in that literal heaven located geographically above or beyond the biosphere.

Beneath the rock of earth was *sheol* – not hell. *Sheol,* viewed as some sort of gray netherworld, was thought to contain the souls of those who had died. God ruled the earth from a literal, physical throne found in heaven, while earth and *sheol* were physical places that contained lesser beings.

Is it possible that the ancient theory that names heaven as geographic is accurate? Or, is heaven spiritual only, vacant of address?

Several years ago I read that physicists now regard the physical world as being comprised of forty-something dimensions or universes. Given the right circumstances, it is possible for immeasurable pieces from this dimension to translate their existence into the dimension next door, much like, as one physicist described it, air passing through a screen door. The screen prevents you and me as complex physical beings from passing through, but the screen makes it possible for *some objects* to translate.

What if heaven is located physically in one of these dimensions next-door, or *as* one of these dimensions?

Heaven closer to you than an atom's breath, and perhaps that is what Jesus meant when he claimed that the kingdom of heaven is among you. Literally, it is in your midst, a part of your unity or your community. Perhaps Jesus meant that the kingdom of heaven exists right here, in some incomprehensible universe side by side with ours, only unlike ours, heaven exists as both incorrupt and incorruptible.

The human soul dedicated to God lives simultaneously in both kingdoms, that of this universe and that of the one next door. Your soul draws its breath from heaven, even while your body is tethered to earth. Heaven and earth are not time-bound or sequential homes in the life of the Christian, but exist simultaneously. You don't enter heaven at some time in the future, after death, but now, moment by moment, choice by choice, and grace by grace. God has already translated you, is translating you, and will continue to translate you, and the only remaining question is: to what degree will you allow translation while you are still alive, here physically on this earth? Will you live as though in heaven?

Thy Kingdom come, thy will be done, on earth as it is in heaven. The mission of people of faith is to translate heaven to earth, to facilitate heaven in its mission to permeate the great divide separating the universes. We become, then, air conduits, the screen door, if you will, through which the air passes.

Jesus repeated this aphorism so often that one might be tempted to take it literally: *The last will be first and the first last.* Perhaps, Jesus never intended this aphorism to be taken as more than a reminder – a reminder of the tension holding our lives together. Maybe it isn't so much that the first will be last sequentially, but rather, simultaneously. You think you're first, but you're just as likely last. The rich are poor, and those who busy themselves thanking God that they are better than, say the homeless person on the street, have already *become* homeless. God sees the homeless person as rich, and the rich person as homeless. Tension, but God sees our world from a different vantage point, so very differently from the way we see it. Thy kingdom come, and what does it mean to bring God's kingdom to earth?

When Jesus was about to tell the unsettling parable of workers in the vineyard, the one in which everybody receives the same *daily* wage, Jesus – or could it have been Matthew? – reminded those listening: *Many that are first shall be last; and the last shall be first.* (Matt. 19:30, KJV) Jesus repeated himself after telling the parable: *So the last shall be first, and the first last: for many be called, but few chosen.* (Matt. 20:16, KJV)

The parable is the story of workers who have no money to feed their families. Hoping someone will hire them, they wait at the marketplace. The marketplace is like a labor convenience store where landowners go to hire temp employees, also known as day laborers.

I used to live just south of the town of San Rafael, California. In San Rafael, undocumented workers hang about in one of two places hoping that someone will hire them for day work: at the front of a strip-mall on a busy street where many cars pass each day, and at the entrance to the local Home Depot where construction foremen purchase materials. These mostly men work for cash which they need to pay rent, feed children and support parents back home. I've often wondered what these workers think of those of us driving by, or whether they notice us at all. I don't speak Spanish very well – a poor excuse, but I've never hired one of these men. Nor have I taken time with them.

Jesus' landowner took time with these men. He hired the undocumented workers to gather his grapes and weed his fields. He took the risk nobody else would take, that these men might be unskilled and incapable of completing, or worse – unwilling to complete – the job for which they were hired. To be sure, hiring the men for the *usual daily wage* appears to be *quid pro quo;* both landowner and worker need something from the other, and thus each of them benefited from the arrangement. But the landowner risked his crop by hiring and trusting these men. And hiring more. And more, yet again.

Who did Jesus imagine was first? The worker hired first or the worker paid first? Which was the last? The worker hired last or the worker paid last? Where is the reversal?

Jesus never answered these questions. The tone of the parable suggests that the men hired early, who started work at sunrise, or 6am or *prime,* were first and would be last. The second group started work at the third hour, 9am, or *terce,* and the third group at the sixth hour, noon, or *sext,* and so-on. *I will pay you whatever is right,* the owner promised each of these workers.

Whatever is right, and I wonder what might have happened had this man not paid some sort of minimum wage? What if his version of "fair" was not the same as their version of "fair?" Did they have legal recourse? They were workers, and the landowner was – well, the landowner. The power differential seems to be too great to have afforded the workers recourse had they needed it. Moreover, their commercial agreement was not in writing and largely unenforceable in a modern court of law.

The prophets spoke vehemently against people in power who would take advantage of those holding an inferior power position. In the old days, one obtained justice at the city gates, but whose word counted most? By the time of Jesus, Scripture hints that a Roman citizen held more power than your typical Galilean.

Would local law have given preferential treatment to the landowner or to the worker? Would the power of the union of day laborers been stronger than that of the landowner? Or vice versa? Who knows, but the day laborers either trusted this landowner or were so desperate for work that they worked regardless of outcome. (One might ask the same of the person becoming a Christian – is it because the person *believes* that facilitates conversion? Or, does it matter to God what motivates a person?)

What about those workers hired at the end of the day? Did they expect to receive minimum wage? Would minimum wage for just one or two hours of work have been enough to purchase bread for a family of children? Why did the landowner wait until the end of the day to hire these men? Was it charity? So they could feed their children, or was it because the grapes were so ripe that, if not picked immediately, their value would have been lost? I've tasted grapes left on the vine too long; they had turned tannic.

Five times that day the landowner hired workers, at *sext,* and *none,* and finally just an hour before *vespers,* the end of daylight. The *vespers* workers were hired last but ordered to line-up first for pay. Why did the landowner make those hired first and who had worked in the hot sun all day long wait the longest to receive their pay, if not to pay them more than the neophytes? Nonetheless, the landowner paid all of them the same thing, the *usual daily wage.* (Matt. 20:2)

Why does the landowner pay those hired last a full day's wage? Wouldn't such generosity encourage sloth? Why would anybody attempt to find work at daybreak if he could wait until noon, do half the job, yet earn the same amount of money? The men hired last worked for about one hour and should have received just one hour's pay, or one-twelfth of the *usual daily wage.* Moreover, one-twelfth is exactly what the landowner had promised to pay these latecomers, when he said he would pay them *whatever is right.* They contracted for *whatever is right,* not the *usual daily wage.* (Matt. 20:4)

Is it conceivable that *whatever is right* is *the usual daily wage* for each person, regardless of time spent working?

And so it was. The landowner paid each of the workers exactly the same amount, which in real terms meant each worker received pay according to a different pay scale. The *vesper* workers received $100 per hour, while the *sext* workers received only $8.33 per hour ($100 divided by 12). Surely the landowner was intelligent enough to appreciate the longer-term problem he was creating by paying workers according to a variable rate. Like so many employment problems, the issue is one of expectations. The landowner was playing with workers' expectations. The *sext* workers, those hired first and working the longest, watched the latecomers receive what they expected to be paid. Because they had worked longer, they adjusted their expectations upward.

They imagined themselves to be the lucky ones – hired first, having worked the longest, and to be rewarded the most, by this most generous man. Twice the *usual daily wage*, they had already spent the extra money in their minds. Maybe they could take tomorrow off and spend time with their wives and kids. But the landowner stuck by the contract and paid them the quite fair *usual daily wage*. Because of their inflated expectations and their exhaustion at having worked in the hot sun all day, these men grew agitated. They grumbled against the *good man* (KJV) of the house. It just isn't fair.

It *isn't* fair. The last should be last, and the first should be first.

The landowner had appropriated Marxian labor economics: *from each according to his ability; to each according to his need*. The late workers were available only late. The all-day workers were available all day. Each worker needed just enough to feed his hungry children. None earned enough to save forward. None earned enough to plan ahead.

Recall Moses and *manna*, and the daily bread of the wandering Hebrew children. Each day just enough manna fell to provide each hungry person enough food for that day only. The Hebrew who tried to save manna for the following day learned the unfortunate lesson that stored manna spoils, and rotten. I shall collect more manna, therefore I shall have more. I shall work twice as long, therefore I shall receive twice the pay.

On a personal note, I am often the *sext* worker hired at 6am who works all day, bearing the heat of the day. I hold work and responsibility as two crucibles, and although I'm past earning salvation from a religious standpoint, I still believe that the responsible person chooses to make something of herself in life. Not so much the slacker. If I'm going to work hard, shouldn't I be entitled to reap the benefits that flow naturally from my work? Perhaps the landowner worked hard to build his business and felt exactly the same way. In fact, Jesus himself seems to say exactly that, that hard work pays off, immediately preceding this parable.

Jesus was speaking to the so-called "rich young ruler," advising him to dispose of everything[13] in order to inherit life. *Sell all that you have.* The disciples became incredulous, and Peter asked, *Who then can be saved?* (Matt. 19:25, KJV) Jesus answered Peter with linchpin advice that provides the interpretation to these several chapters: *For [people], it is impossible; but with God all things are possible.* (Matt. 19:26)

All things are possible, but Jesus' answer upset Peter. He, like I, was a responsible man. Peter was hired at daybreak, and by the end of it all, he would have worked throughout the entire metaphoric day. He would have given up his entire life for the kingdom. Almost in anticipation of both his life and his death, Peter asked, *We have given up everything and followed you. What will there be for us?* (Matt. 20:27, NASB)

When I was in college, I joined a nondenominational evangelical church. The charismatic nature of the worship and congregation were vivacious, offering such life and hope and salvation. Peoples' lives were arrested, altered, and faith-infused. The problem was, there was no halfway, because the Jesus of my evangelical days would not have hired anybody at noonday. You were either in or out, but never both. You were hired at 6am or not at all. The head of the church used to preach, *Jesus is either Lord of all, or not Lord at all.*

Before you find that line offensive, you might want to recall that Jesus said essentially the same thing: *you can't serve two masters, God and money.* And at another point, when Jesus promised people they would be turned away at the end of the age, he added, *depart from me, I never knew you.* There is an unsavory part to Jesus' message that insists upon separation of wheat from chaff and sheep from goats.

---

[13] In Matthew, Mark and Luke, the man is rich. In Matthew, the man is young. In Luke, the man is a ruler. Nowhere is the man simultaneously rich, young, and a ruler.

You are either in or out. You can't have it both ways. The standard is impossible, but Peter reminded Jesus, I've met the standard: *I am loyal. I gave up everything.*

Jesus answered Peter obliquely with an obscure promise about sitting on twelve thrones judging twelve tribes. (Matt. 19:28) (One must assume Jesus did not intend to include Judas Iscariot in his tally of twelve – Judas, the man about whom Jesus would later observe it would have been better had he not been born. (Matt. 26:24) Either that or grace far exceeds my expectation.)

Peter wanted to take Jesus literally. *What about us? We've left everything.* The early workers were literal like Peter. They started first thing in the morning, so they deserved the most. The last shall be first. Perhaps you appreciate the dangers of being literal with malleable Scripture.

Isn't the point something like this? None of life with God works the way you think it should. And you think, of course, of yourself as the same character in the story who I think I am, the worker hired first. Only, someone out there has to be the one who was hired last. Someone was hired at the end of the day. Someone *needs* the same amount of grace that the rest of us have received, and perhaps more – just to be able to feed small children. Who gets to say who is first? Or who is last?

The landowner was not unfair. He was not unjust. He respected responsibility and paid the early men the wage he had promised and they had earned.

The landowner was also charitable. Charity, as in love. As in *caritas,* the love of God. *Caritas* is love so wide and deep that it encompasses even those who cannot make a perfect commitment to Jesus as lord of all. Who find themselves unable to let go, to sell all they have, and give the money to the poor. The one who cannot find his way to the marketplace at break of dawn, and are lucky to have made it by five pm.

This story of the landowner and his employees has everything to do with the interaction between Jesus and the *rich young ruler,* as well as the segue conversation between Jesus and his disciples, linking these two stories.

The rich young man wanted to know what he should "do," which is, in the end, his inherent problem. Faith is not about what you do. You can work all day long, and even three straight days, and never earn more of heaven than the person who starts work at the end of the third day. Manna is manna, and grace is grace, both wholly sufficient substances. An ounce equals a pound, and a pound equals an ounce, and both sate a person completely. There is always enough grace to go around, yet just enough grace to go around. Nobody goes hungry with the dispensation of grace; however, you cannot horde it for tomorrow. Relying, you see, on past grace is not relying on grace at all.

What must I do? When the rich young man called Jesus "Good Master," you can feel Jesus bristling. *God alone is good,* Jesus answered curtly. (Mark 10:18)

Jesus isn't good? Of course he – Jesus – is good, but not inherently good. He is good because God is coursing through his soul like blood through veins. A good man does not need grace and does not need to rely upon God. None of us – not even Jesus – is sufficient in and of himself. The man's statement harkens back to the garden of self-sufficiency that became Adam and Eve's downfall.

Nonetheless, the *rich young ruler* tried so very hard to explain his own goodness, his Eden-like self-sufficiency. He had done it all, kept every commandment, honored his father and mother and even loved his neighbor as himself.

Loved his neighbor as himself. He probably cooked at the local soup kitchen, served on the church vestry, and hired workers he didn't really need so that their children would not go to sleep hungry. If there was anybody who was *good*, it was this man. But this man would not have asked the question, *what must I do,* if he had really believed deep down that he was good *enough*. Being so-called *good* had failed him, and completely. At best, the being-good philosophy made him a decent human being, but in the deeper matters of the soul – in the question, *Who are you, O God, and*

Who am I? – being *good* is moot. Where is God? Who is God? Why do I feel inadequate?

There *is* this hole in the human heart that only God can fill.[14] To put it another way, *Listen! I am standing at the door knocking: if you hear my voice and open the door, I will come in to you and eat with you, and you with me.* (Rev. 3:20)

Jesus answered the young man, matching answer for question: *If you want to be perfect, go sell your possessions, and give the money to the poor ....* (Matt. 19:21) Only, the man asked the wrong question. It isn't about what you can or must do. It is about posture, yours with God's. Maybe the better question might be that St. Francis question, recited previously, *Who are you, O God, and who am I?*

Jesus nonetheless answered the question the man asked, not the one he should have asked. If you *must do* something, then do this – help the poor. You can never go wrong helping people in need.

You and I are eavesdroppers, listening to a conversation meant for both one and many, for both the *rich young ruler* and us. The heart of the matter for us is the question never asked.

Money and the poor are red herring issues. Jesus cared about the poor and our relationship with money, but he could just as quickly turn callous regarding both. When the critics complained about the woman wasting expensive perfume by pouring it across Jesus' head – *this ointment could have been sold for a large sum and the money given to the poor* –, Jesus answered, *you always have the poor with you, but you will not always have me.* (Matt. 26:6-13) It isn't that Jesus hates the poor, or thinks you and I should ignore people begging for money on the street. Indeed, the poor person you encounter may find himself first in line at the pearly gates. The

---

[14] "What else does this craving, and this helplessness, proclaim but that there was once in man a true happiness, of which all that now remains is the empty print and trace? This he tries in vain to fill with everything around him, seeking in things that are not there the help he cannot find in those that are, though none can help, since this infinite abyss can be filled only with an infinite and immutable object; in other words by God himself."
– Blaise Pascal, *Pensées* VII(425)

last will be first. And perhaps you recall Jesus at the Sermon on the Mount praising the poor in spirit. Moral theologians speak to God's *preference* for the poor, a concept deeply rooted in Scripture and Christian tradition. Jesus *is* concerned for the poor, *is* concerned about the men hired late in the day. Is concerned when people go hungry and sleep outside exposed to the elements, or are lost in a sea of alcohol and depression, all poor of soul. Jesus *is* equally concerned that a *rich young ruler* is rudderless in life, adrift in his sea of confusion. Jesus is concerned for *us all*.

The *rich young ruler* was hiking on the wrong trail, and all he had as guide was this vague sense of ennui.

What else must I do? You can't *do* anything. Not a damn thing. To receive Grace. If you want to be perfect – if perfection is your goal – fine. Go ahead and purchase moral perfection. Sell all you have and give it to those who have not. But there is no love in that, no *caritas,* or Christian charity. Your self-sacrifice is a mere sacrifice for self. You hope to find entrance to the kingdom, so you ask about method. Only, there is no method. There is no formula. Even the Southern Baptist formula (adapted from Paul) of believing in your heart and confessing with your mouth Jesus as Lord is a formula that has failed way too many people, for you see, every single formula risks becoming method – rather than being an avenue to faith. Reliance upon a formula is reliance upon self. It will not work. Only relying upon God will work. Faith in self is not the faith of Jesus.

The first shall be last and the last first is not prescriptive. It is descriptive. It is this parable of the landowner, which plainly says: there are no rules upon which you can rely except the rule that there are no rules. Rely only upon God. God saves, not anything else upon which you may attempt to stake your claim – the commandments (like the rich young ruler), leaving it all and making Jesus *lord of all* (like the disciples) or working all day long rather than just part of the day (the workers).

The landowner walked through the marketplace full of compassion, sad at finding displaced workers still unemployed.

He knew their children would go hungry that night, if he did not do something. He knew these men shared the same ennui as the aimless rich young man. This landowner was a man of grace, a man who distributed the commodity of grace freely to those in need.

And the rich young man? *If you want to be perfect* … well, go ahead and try. The irony? perfection of soul comes not by doing, but by being. So keep on trying; see how much you earn at the end of the day.

Chapter 4

The Blessings of a Man whose Friends are Good

When [Jesus] returned to Capernaum after some days, it was reported that he was at home. So many gathered around that there was no longer room for them, not even in front of the door; and he was speaking the word to them. Then some people came, bringing to him a paralyzed man, carried by four of them. And when they could not bring him to Jesus because of the crowd, they removed the roof above him; and after having dug through it, they let down the mat on which the paralytic lay. When Jesus saw their faith, he said to the paralytic, "Son, your sins are forgiven." Now some of the Scribes were sitting there, questioning in their hearts, "Why does this fellow speak in this way? It is blasphemy! Who can forgive sins but God alone?" At once Jesus perceived in his spirit that they were discussing these questions among themselves; and he said to them, "Why do you raise such questions in your hearts? Which is easier, to say to the paralytic, 'Your sins are forgiven,' or to say, 'Stand up and take your mat and walk'? But so that you may know that the Son of Man has authority on earth to forgive sins"—he said to the paralytic— "I say to you, stand up, take your mat and go to your home." And he stood up, and immediately took the mat and went out before all of them; so that they were all amazed and glorified God, saying, "We have never seen anything like this!" Mark 2:1-12.

Story Characters

Paralytic – The paralytic man is a prop; his faith is irrelevant to healing.
Crowd – Crazed, enamored with Jesus as pop star, pressing in on Jesus.

Jesus – "Who is this?" You think you know, but you have never seen anything like this!
Scribes – Insincere questioners.
Four men – Friends whose dominant faith is responsible for healing the paralytic.
The Message – "word spread that he was back at home …"

Point of the Story: The Scribes connected sickness to sin, assuming that illness and/or incapacity were evidence that someone had misbehaved. *Ironically,* Jesus acquiesced to their flawed philosophy, but healed the paralytic anyway. The conclusion? Perhaps God is less interested in sin than most people believe.

I grew up during the 1960's. I recall watching black and white newsreels of the Beatles' first tour in America. Mobs of crazed teenaged girls crowded the lips of concert stages, their arms stretched out in charismatic worship. The girls screamed their praise, swooning, bodies and souls swaying carelessly.

I've wondered over the years, whatever happened to those girls? What kind of women did they grow into? Mothers whose daughters later crowded stages at the feet of some eighties punk rock band? Maybe the girls as adults became embarrassed when recalling their youthful displays of public adoration? Or the opposite, proud of their participation in a movement that ultimately altered the cultural direction of the country and world? These young women might have crushed the Beatles, had the police not intervened.

Jesus seems to have left Capernaum because he had become famous. Why had Jesus become famous? What was attracting so many people to Jesus? Was it the miracles? The holiness they sensed emanating from him? Or, were people simply bored? Nothing good to watch was on TV, so to speak.

Generally speaking, people relate better to externals than they do to internals, to the physical more than to the spiritual. Jesus' healing miracles impressed people, but his miracles pointed to an internal purity. Jesus was unlike any other religious personality they had ever experienced; he embodied *true* religion, not just in external practice, but internally. Jesus, they sensed, was a man of integrity. He talked the talk because he walked the walk. Jesus was real, and people in a world defined by false truths and fake people clamor for anything that might be real.

Yet, even in the face of the person Jesus, the people could not apprehend or fathom the ionic structure of the man. Who is this man, who even the winds and the seas obey? (Mk. 8, Matt. 4) Following one incident, a menacing demon identified Jesus, *I know who you are, the Holy One of God* (Mk. 1:24). Yet, Jesus forbade other devils from disclosing his identity. (Mk. 1:34) Most people are desperate to be seen for who they are, to be noticed. Yet this man hid his identity, tucked it away from the public view. Who does that? What kind of man is this?

Mark tells the reader (or listener) what kind of man this is in his very beginning, the Son of God. *The beginning of the Good News of the Son of God*. Mark repeats Jesus' identity mere verses later when that mystical voice from heaven speaks to Jesus at his baptism: *You are my son.*

The crowds cannot read Mark's initial verse, nor can they hear the Father's voice. Hence, you as reader know at the outset, but the crowds in Mark's story do not. Yet, they sensed something unique, some cultural and religious shift occasioned by raw truth, and they flocked to Jesus.

But Jesus viewed his mission as being one to all of Galilee, so he left Capernaum, the place of so much adulation, for parts unknown. (Mk. 1:38, 39) Now Jesus has returned, and the story of the paralytic unfolds. Word spread fast, and the crowd mobs Jesus to such a degree that the doorway to the house is sealed by people. Not even one more person can squeeze into the house, and certainly not this man hauled on a stretcher by four friends.

But these friends are friends indeed, tenacious and loyal. How far have they lugged this *pallet man* to Jesus? City blocks? Miles? Through multiple villages? The crowd blocks the doorway into the house, so the men must heave the man onto the roof and break a hole through it. They lower their friend like an angel down, right in front of Jesus. To face Jesus. So Jesus will have tell this man to his face that he cannot be healed. They surmise.

The so-called American version of the "prosperity gospel" is nothing new. It is founded upon this haunting yet ages-old precept: God is well-pleased with people who do good or obey law or live somehow better lives than other people. God rewards or "blesses" good people with health and financial stability – prosperity. Their faith and goodness incarnate through wallets and possessions. When you give money away, you receive a bigger house, bigger 401(k), and a prosperous business.

The converse applies equally. The person who is not good, who does not do obey the law of God, who does not please God, is accursed, and is thus more than likely to lead a life full of physical and/or fiscal ailment.

The corollary to the prosperity gospel is perhaps obvious: being rich and/or in good health means that God has blessed you. God has blessed you because you are fundamentally good. (Or, good at faith, at being properly religious.) Being poor or in bad health indicates that God has withheld blessing you because you are fundamentally *not* good. (Or, you might be a person who is bad at faith or not properly religious.) The state of your bank account and your health are barometers of the state of your moral and/or religious soul.

In fact, the contours of life prove just how faulty the prosperity gospel is. Very faithful Christians suffer the travails of life just like unfaithful people. The rain falls on the just and the unjust. Bad things happen to good people, and good things happen to bad people. Good things, bad things, shit happens. Successful Christians file for bankruptcy protection while people of questionable faith or morals possess burgeoning portfolios. Good people do not necessarily win election to public office, and we all know people of questionable moral character who have won election to the highest office in the land. The product of life judges the prosperity gospel harshly; that "gospel" wants for truth deeper.

Why try, then, to be fair? Just? Faithful? Responsible?

In fact, living a responsible life *inclines* one toward security, while living an irresponsible life *inclines* one towards insecurity. Smoking early in life is more likely to cause problems later in life than not ever smoking. But the proverb is proverbial, not absolute. There is no guarantee of absolute security in life, any more than there is of insecurity. Sometimes life just happens. Sometimes, the unjust man wins the lottery while the just man falls into financial ruin. Moreover, the goal of life is depth of soul, not a fat pocketbook or good health.

When it comes to faith, neither financial state (rich or poor) matters – not really. Whether I am rich or I am poor, I will serve the Lord. Whether I am in good health or ill health, I will serve the Lord. *Though he slay me, I will hope in him.* (Job 13:15, Jer.) Who was it who said, *I have been rich, and I have been poor. I never let either condition affect my standard of living.*

In Jesus' day, people viewed physical disability as indicia of God's disfavor. Someone *must* have sinned, otherwise this person would not be suffering. (*See, e.g.,* John 9:2) Thus, by forgiving the pallet man's sin before healing him, Jesus appears to fall into the trap of the prosperity gospel. The man must need his sins to be forgiven. Is this what Mary and Joseph taught Jesus growing up? Or had they introduced Jesus to a different God, one who is three-dimensional and not two?

Who has faith? Certainly not the man paralyzed. He just lays there, on his pallet, watching his four prove their faith by action. Devoted, they are determined to help this man. You can tell; they do not treat their friend as though he has sinned. At worst, the man's so-called sinful life is a distraction to his friends, a sideshow, one they choose to ignore. Were it otherwise, they would have left the man rotting in the sewers along with the other beggars. *Throw me a scrap, a coin, anybody, please help.*

No, these men treat their friend with human dignity. They are deeply sad, lamentatious, even, at his plight. *Love believes all things*, and they believe in the man himself, that he is, at root, good. Their faith takes flight on the wings not of God, nor of Jesus, but of their own love. They ignore the house crammed with people, climb the roof, cut a hole in the roof, and let the man down – for one and only one reason. That he might, perhaps just might, be healed.

Jesus observes their love for the man; he is *astonished* by their devotion to him.

Jesus *cares* to heal people. Like the leper who said to Jesus, *If you want to, you can cure me,* to which Jesus responded, *Of course I want to.* Now Jesus answers the press of these four devoted friends who lower the man to Jesus: *Of course I want to heal your friend.* Of course I want to see him whole, this man fractured and cursed by devil and life.

And there it is. This man does not pray the confession; he does not ask his sins to be forgiven. Nor do his friends so much as hint at the presence of sins requiring absolution. Their collaborative faith has nothing to do with sin or forgiveness. And Jesus: who could possibly think that Jesus is linking sin to sickness? Is this man bankrupt either because he has lived a bad life or lacks faith?

Enter the Scribes. Supercilious, condemning Jesus for "forgiving sins," when all the man really wants is to be healed. Jesus, you see, in this ironic twist, plays *their* game, forgiving the man's sins, and by doing so, Jesus brings the issue to the fore – not the issue of faith or forgiveness or whether bad things happen only to bad people – but the issue of identity. Only God can forgive sins, which is the foundation upon which the Scribes have built their unspoken complaint against Jesus. Only God can forgive, so who do you think you are, forgiving this man's sins?

They mock Jesus, but Jesus mocks them in return. Jesus declines argument and instead heals the man. Were he to engage their argument, he might instruct them about their fundamental God-given responsibility to forgive the sins of others. Not just God's responsibility, but theirs. After all, did Jesus not believe that we *must* forgive in order to receive forgiveness? (*cf.* The Lord's Prayer)

No, rather than argue with the Scribes, Jesus heals the man. *Take up your pallet and walk.* Translated into Scribe-language, Jesus' words mean this: your sins are forgiven. The Scribes' understanding of a tight-assed God who holds people accountable line upon line is debunked. Not by argument, but by action. Essentially, Jesus is telling the Scribes: *take your theory of sin and shove it.*

Yes, Jesus says to the paralyzed man, *Take up your pallet and walk.* Jesus words here echo this parallel imperative, *Take up your cross and follow.* Your pallet is not your pallet, nor is the cross yours. Did you read correctly? Your cross is not your cross – and the truism that you have to endure hardship in order to gain is not absolute, after all. Jesus bore the cross, and the man on the pallet was healed. The man carried a pallet he no longer needed. It had been laden heavy with his dead weight, but it weighs comparatively little, now, just like your cross weighs comparatively little in light of the burden Jesus bore for you on his own cross. Dead weight, yours.

Regardless, Jesus is sticking the dog's nose in his own poop. The Scribes believe that bad things really do happen to bad people, just because they are bad, that sin and not circumstance cause deformity. Here, Scribes, take this – *your sins are forgiven.* But which is easier? To state forgiveness, or to prove it by healing? These are their terms, their poop, but Jesus heals the man to prove one thing: that the man's sins – whatever they might be – were forgiven a long time ago.

Or, perhaps, Jesus heals the man simply because he loves the man just like he loved the leper: *Of course I want to heal you.* Jesus wants nothing more than to heal and to restore and to forgive and to grace. Take up your pallet and walk.

Everyone means everyone, and Mark writes that everyone becomes astounded at the healing. Including the Scribes. Dumbfounded, jaws drop open while they watch the forgiven and healed man pack in his pallet and walk away through a crowd parted like the Red Sea. A man of obvious sin, think the Scribes, incongruously healed. Jesus *does* have the power to forgive sins. If sins cause his sickness. Which they do not. Which is the point. Sickness is sickness.

This man's friends must be cheering from the rooftop, literally jumping down off the roof to join the man leaving. Skipping and dancing and praising God.

But darkness permeates the Scribes' overcast sky, a flash of lightning, a clap of thunder. In Capernaum just verses before, Mark writes that Jesus taught with authority, *unlike the Scribes*. (Mk. 1:22) Authority, and isn't there an extraordinary sense of purity to Jesus' authority and teaching, how he organizes himself while healing? Authority, not of the Scribes, for they speak, but without the mystical presence of God Almighty. Jesus, in contradistinction, speaks in the person of God. *Who is this who even the winds and seas obey?* they wonder. God's Son, the beloved.

Authority and forgiveness and the surprise of the ages. Jesus, a man of integrity, his faith being a lived faith.

Chapter 5

You Give them Something to Eat

The apostles gathered around Jesus, and told him all that they had done and taught. He said to them, "Come away to a deserted place all by yourselves and rest a while." For many were coming and going, and they had no leisure even to eat. And they went away in the boat to a deserted place by themselves. Now many saw them going and recognized them, and they hurried there on foot from all the towns and arrived ahead of them. As he went ashore, he saw a great crowd; and he had compassion for them, because they were like sheep without a shepherd; and he began to teach them many things. When it grew late, his disciples came to him and said, "This is a deserted place, and the hour is now very late; send them away so that they may go into the surrounding country and villages and buy something for themselves to eat." But he answered them, "You give them something to eat." They said to him, "Are we to go and buy two hundred denarii worth of bread, and give it to them to eat?" And he said to them, "How many loaves have you? Go and see." When they had found out, they said, "Five, and two fish." Then he ordered them to get all the people to sit down in groups on the green grass. So they sat down in groups of hundreds and of fifties. Taking the five loaves and the two fish, he looked up to heaven, and blessed and broke the loaves, and gave them to his disciples to set before the people; and he divided the two fish among them all. And all ate and were filled; and they took up twelve baskets full of broken pieces and of the fish. Those who had eaten the loaves numbered five thousand men. Mark 6:30-44. (*See also, Matt. 14:13-21, Lk. 9:10-17, Jn. 6:1-13; cf. Mk. 8:1-10*)

According to Mark, Jesus fed 10-15,000[15] people with five loaves of bread and two fish. (Mk. 6:30-44) He fed 8-10,000 people with seven loaves of bread and just a few small fish. (Mk. 8:1-10)

The first feeding took place at the end of a long day during which Jesus taught the crowds in that remote "lonely place." The second feeding took place at the end of three days, among people also far from home. The first feeding followed Jesus' teaching the people. The second feeding took place after the people had "been with Jesus," with no reference to teaching. The first feeding took place in response to the disciples' concern about the people's hunger. The second feeding took place in response to Jesus' concern.

To accomplish the first feeding, Jesus asked the disciples to group the people, which they did, into hundreds and fifties. To accomplish the second feeding, Jesus instructed the people as a "crowd," without grouping them.

In both instances: the people sat on the ground; Jesus took whatever food was available and blessed it, in the first instance by raising his eyes to heaven, and in the second by offering thanks; Jesus broke the bread; his disciples distributed the bread; and every person present ate until full.

After the people ate, the disciples collected twelve basketsful left over for the first feeding,[16] and seven for the second.[17]

Well before both feedings, Jesus had sent his twelve disciples out on mission in pairs, giving them authority over unclean spirits. For sustenance, they were to rely upon God. Jesus told them not to take anything with them for the trip, except their staff: no bread; no haversack; no spare tunic; and no coppers for your purse. Your trust will give you purchase. Enter houses when invited, and stay until it is time to leave. When you are not listened to or welcomed, shake the dust off your feet as a sign to them. (Mk. 6:7-13)

---

[15] Extrapolation. Scripture notes 5,000 men (*plus women and children*).
[16] A reference to the twelve tribes of Israel? To the twelve disciples?
[17] A reference to the number of perfection or the number of God?

Shake the dust off your feet, and if I'm not mistaken – although I have been unable to find the exact quote – Madeleine L'Engle once interpreted this shaking of the dust as non-judgmental. It is descriptive, and means no more than this: *God will send someone else to you.*[18] Someone you *will* listen to.

When I was nineteen years old and in college at Auburn University, I relied upon a University food credit card to survive. I would use this card to live beyond my then current means, which were, at best, meager. The card enabled me to spend future income presently.

One day, I had this overwhelming sense that God wanted me to stop relying on that credit card for sustenance. Now, I am not and was not in the habit of imagining God telling me this or that on any type of regular basis. These many years later, I can count on no more than both hands the occasions I've sensed the Holy Spirit guiding me the way it did on that particular day, not as a gentle dove but as a commanding presence. The direction was real, not imagined, more like a gnawing at the soul or a grating whisper, than a gentle breeze.

I've felt the Holy Spirit as a gentle breeze far more often. One day, working at the church office, I felt a nudge to call a particular parish family, one I'd not spent any time with other than on the rare Sunday mornings they would attend church. When I called, the husband answered the phone. I greeted him, *Hi, John. This is Rob at the church. I wanted to check in with you and Bernice to see how things are going.*

Before I finished the sentence, John interrupted me. *I can't believe you're calling*, he said, his voice shaky. *We just got home from the store.* John was crying. Something was wrong. *We ran over our dog. In the driveway.*

John and Bernice lived with their baby boy on a farm with a long driveway. The dog had run out in front of the car to greet them, but they did not see him. The dog jumped under the front right

---

[18] See L'Engle, Madeleine. Bright Evening Star. Shaw Books (2001).

wheel. Now, because of the grace of that gentle breeze, I had the opportunity to comfort John. I do not recall what was said next, but I do recall experiencing an overwhelming sense of awe at God and Spirit and my very small place in the universe, and of coincidences that you know *are not* coincidences. God exchanged desperate grace for this family's desperate grief.

But at Auburn, that day, the voice was anything but gentle – haunting and clear and God's.

I really *was* a poor college student. My father died when I was 18, and I barely survived on Social Security, which was available in those days to college students whose breadwinning parent had died. Part-time work, too, and I lived on about $600 per month – which paid for tuition, room and board.

The voice insisted I tear up the food credit card – to rely no longer on credit, but on God, for support. Crazy-making thoughts. God? Stupid faith? The devil? But the thought rankled me. Tormented by grace and God, I relented and cut the card in half. I didn't have any money, not even enough to buy food that day. And I didn't tell a soul.

At the time, I was living in a large house with friends, but we kept our food individually. That morning, I skipped breakfast, as I often did, and returned to the house just in time for lunch. One of my roommates happened to be making soup and asked whether I might like some. *Yes*, I answered, relieved. After lunch, the mail came. And – you guessed it – there was a check in the mail for $200 from my home church in Florida, the proceeds of a scholarship that I had not applied for and did not know existed.

Miracles and blind trust, and the disciples were likewise instructed by Jesus to make no provision for themselves. When they returned, Jesus did not ask them, nor did they tell him, how they had managed to survive. They had no school credit card. Instead, the disciples regaled Jesus with stories of people being healed, and how they found themselves teaching like Jesus would, to multitudes and with power. Food turns out to have been a distraction, a sideshow, something necessary but not the focus.

Do you eat to live, or live to eat?

The Gospel told by John offers a glimpse into Jesus' understanding of food as a mere sideshow. Jesus was too busy to eat, so the disciples pressed food on him. He responded, *I have food to eat that you do not know about.* (Jn. 4:32) And then, *My food is to do the will of Him who sent me, and to complete his work.* (Jn. 4:34)

This deeply spiritual message is exactly what Jesus hoped to convey that first day when he told the disciples to feed the people. The disciples had expressed concern about physical hunger, while Jesus wanted to feed the people spiritual grace.

But before all this, the disciples were tired from their own mission. As any preacher can tell you, preaching kingdom can be taxing. The effective preacher donates a piece of his soul to those listening. Jesus understood the disciples' need to rest and recoup. *Come away to a lonely place by yourselves and rest for a while.*

But people followed them and pressed in on them. Jesus had just as much compassion for the people as he had for his disciples, seeing them as sheep without a shepherd. Jesus taught them – "at some length" (Mk. 6:35, Jer.), and by the end of the day, the people had grown physically hungry, and the disciples yet more exhausted. The disciples noted the people's hunger and urged Jesus to send them away, perhaps duplicitously.

For the disciples *were* exhausted. They had not rested. And they, like the people, were also physically hungry. Knowing this miracle-working Jesus the way they did, the disciples probably worried that Jesus would put the people's needs before their own. *Why doesn't Jesus stop teaching and let the people go home so they can eat?* Let them leave this lonely place; it has no grocery store.

A lonely or *thin* place is a physical place where the veil between this world and the spiritual barely divides. Your soul obtains spiritual nourishment in lonely places. Where did Jesus go when he felt depleted? To a lonely place.

And he did, so often, feel depleted. Like the time he healed the woman with a hemorrhage. The crowd was pressing in from all sides. And when the woman with the hemorrhage touched him and was instantly healed, Jesus *felt* power leave him. (Mark 5:30)

This first miracle of the loaves, the disciples' rest had to wait.

The second miracle of the loaves was different from the first. (*See* Mark 8) This time Jesus felt compassion because he could tell the people were physically hungry. The first time, Jesus had seen them differently, as *sheep without a shepherd.* (*cf.* Mark 6:34) Jesus refused to send them away without food, lest they collapse along the way. The disciples became perturbed, knowing there was no food within miles. Whereas the first time, the disciples seemed to care that the people were hungry, this time they do not seem to care. (Mark 8:4)

Nonetheless, Jesus used the disciples to work his miracle, just like he had that first time. The disciples distributed, and just like before, the act of distribution became the miracle. Distribution multiplied the bread. Faith expressed by action, as it so often is. Each person ate just enough, as though the bread were God's manna from heaven. (*See* Exodus 16)

Manna. The ancient Hebrews were hungry people who sounded like little children in the late afternoon. They whined to Moses for leading them out of Egypt without bringing food. They were hungry, so God sent them manna from heaven. God's directions for the operation of the manna miracle were simple. Gather enough manna each morning for that day, and that day only, no more and no less. Fridays and Saturdays will be different from the other days. On Fridays, you will gather enough for two days, Friday plus the Saturday Sabbath, and in that way, you will not have to collect manna on Sabbath. Those who collect more than they need on any given day will soon realize that there is only enough for that one day, while those who collect too little will also realize that they have enough for that one day.

At St. Stephen's Church in Belvedere, California, the Altar Guild bakes fresh communion bread for Sunday services. The Altar Guild is divided into teams, and one baker serves on each team. The one loaf is always sufficient, being neither too much nor too little.

When I served at St. Stephen's, I would sometimes wonder, as I would distribute the bread, whether a larger piece of bread might mean the person receives a larger share of grace. When a small child with eyes full of wonder would gather at the table, hands stretched upward in joy, I would drop a larger chunk of bread into his small hands. The child would invariably look at me with eyes wide, appreciating our conspiracy, that he received more than anybody else at the table. Such joy, but I also wanted each child to understand that, at the table, he or she was and always will be special. Does that child with a larger piece of bread receive the larger piece of grace? Maybe. Maybe joy opens the door to grace.

The disciples felt little joy in either instance of crowd feeding. They were half-baked men of half-faith.

Not long after the second feeding, the disciples were sailing at Jesus' instruction in a boat to the opposite shore. They had forgotten to bring food with them on the boat, to eat on the opposite shore. Later, Jesus warned them against the yeast of Herod and the Pharisees. They assumed Jesus was chastising them for their forgetfulness. But couldn't they recall the fact that Jesus had multiplied loaves and fishes twice? *What have you done for me lately?* Jesus reminded them about feeding the people, and incredulously asked, *Have you eyes that do not see, ears that do not hear ... Are you still without perception?* (Mark 8:18; 21, Jer.)

Without perception. Seeing, but eyes that do not see. To drive the point home, that the disciples were still without perception, Jesus healed a blind man, but partway. He took the man outside of town, spit into his hands, and rubbed spit into the man's eyes, asking, *Can you see anything?*

As discussed earlier, the man *began* seeing, but partway. *I see men as trees walking*, he said. Jesus' only half-miracle, but he persisted. The man finally *saw*. Twenty-twenty.

Following Mark's description of this half-miracle, followed by the full miracle, and also in light of the disciples' boat ride, Jesus asked the disciples about identity. *Who do people say I am?*

They answered Jesus with ethereal imagination, *Elijah,* or *John the Baptist come back to life.*

But who do you say I am? Do you see, or are you still blind?

Still blind, for Peter answered, *You are the Christ.* And then rebuked Jesus for claiming Messiah would have to suffer. Peter spoke truth, but failed to appreciate truth. To perceive it fully.

Peter, and all the disciples are *visibly* blind – and so are we.

Jesus cared for the people. He nourished the first group with spiritual food. The disciples wanted to send them away, ostensibly for food, but just as likely because the disciples themselves were hungry and tired. Jesus told them, *You feed them,* but then Jesus fed them.

The second time, Jesus noticed the hunger of the crowd and wanted to feed the people. The disciples resisted, but Jesus persisted.

Funny, the disciples never missed a meal. They always had access to food. Even on their mission trips, they had seen God attend to their physical needs completely. Why did they not understand either time, at either feeding, that food was not the issue? Never was. Faith was. Faith as seeing.

Faith is seeing what others are blind to. Seeing things that are not there. Seeing not only the physical person of Jesus and his identity as Messiah, but seeing the hand and Spirit of God that flows in and around and through everything. *You feed them,* and they could because they, too, had the same Spirit as Jesus. Only they couldn't *perceive* the gift of God in Jesus or in themselves. They were half-healed people, and so are we.

The people complained to Moses in the wilderness – they had no food – but their complaint was not about food. It was about seeing. The manna was there, just enough, *give us this day our daily bread,* and whether you have a savings account or retirement plan, all God cares about is today. Plan for tomorrow; be prudent. But trust in God. *Today* is the day of salvation. *Just for today,* so the AA slogan goes.

The throngs of people pressed in on Jesus from every side, listening to every word, letting him heal them physically, emotionally and spiritually. For the first time in their lives, they heard someone speak truth about God, and not the red-herring stuff about obeying the sabbath for the sake of the sabbath, or cleaning the outside of the cup while the inside is frothing with germs. The sabbath is for man, and not man for the sabbath. Clean the inside of the cup. It is inside the person that is corrupt, not outside.

These people were not worried about food. They, like Jesus, had food that could not be seen. (*I have food ye know not of,* said Jesus.) They survived on every word that flowed from Jesus' mouth.

Seek first the kingdom, and all these things will be added, and Jesus cared that they might grow hungry, in both instances, and supplied accordingly.

Martha, you worry about so many things, but Mary is concerned about the one that counts.

One thing, and it wasn't to figure out where the next meal might come from, or to find rest. All these things will be added unto you ...

One thing only.

Chapter 6

The Rudeness of Jesus

Syrophoenician Woman: Mark

From there he set out and went away to the region of Tyre. He entered a house and did not want anyone to know he was there. Yet he could not escape notice, but a woman whose little daughter had an unclean spirit immediately heard about him, and she came and bowed down at his feet. Now the woman was a Gentile, of Syrophoenician origin. She begged him to cast the demon out of her daughter. He said to her, "Let the children be fed first, for it is not fair to take the children's food and throw it to the dogs." But she answered him, "Sir, even the dogs under the table eat the children's crumbs." Then he said to her, "For saying that, you may go—the demon has left your daughter." So she went home, found the child lying on the bed, and the demon gone. Mark 7:24-30.

A mostly discarded Christian tradition required the faithful to fast during the hours leading up to *Holy Communion*. I cannot explain how or why this tradition developed, although I did find two clues.

First, an online article dates the practice to third-century Tertullian.[19] Tertullian, it seems, described communion bread as that which should be eaten before all others, the implication being obvious. Meals are taken following, not before, communion.

Second, Scripture provides a similar allusion, only with regard to the wine. According to Paul, Jesus offered the broken bread as

---

[19] See http://canonlawmadeeasy.com/2017/08/31/canon-law-changed-fasting-communion/.

his body prior to the main meal, and he offered the wine as his blood following the main meal. (*See* 1 Cor. 11:23-25)

Neither Tertullian nor Scripture requires fasting before receiving communion. Why, then, require Christians to fast prior to communion? The most obvious reason would be to prepare oneself, to make oneself holier and thus more ready to receive the holiest of sacraments.

Yet, the very nature and act of communion points to human imperfection and the desperate need, precisely because frail, for the person to make contact with the divine. Communion is nothing if not the confluence of human frailty and divine grace.[20] Grace is offered to the needy, not to the perfect; to the *unholy,* not the holy. Grace insists upon infirmity, which is behind Paul's rhetorical question to the Romans: *who will ascend to heaven to bring Christ down?* One simply cannot save oneself. (Rom. 10:6, *para.*)

Hence, fasting prior to communion as a way to *ascend to heaven,* as it were, is superfluous, an add-on, and appears to be an unnecessary embellishment.

There is a similar tradition among priests exercised immediately prior to communion, the *lavabo*. The priest washes her hands prior to handling the elements of communion and offering the holy and Great Thanksgiving.

The acolyte tilts the flagon of water just above the priest's hands. Water pours out of the flagon and across the hands in order to wash them, and then it spills into the *lavabo* bowl beneath, held in the acolyte's other hand. The hands drip water like the soul drips hope, and the priest dries her hands using the pure linen towel draped across the acolyte's forearm. Many priests utter a portion of Psalm 26 as prayer to wash and dry the soul. *I will wash my hands in innocence ...*

---

[20] There can be no such thing as human purity, is there? Each of us is both fallible and failed, in need of extraordinary grace. The act of confession alone, without attending grace, is not helpful.

Like the tradition of fasting prior to taking communion, the tradition of the lavabo seems superfluous. The priest can never wash her hands enough to justify handling what surely must be, in the moment, the purest elements in the universe.

Mosaic Law and Purity

Ancient Mosaic law distinguished people as pure and impure, clean and unclean. The state of impurity or uncleanness came about because of the way a person behaved *or* because a person existed in an unacceptable state – having, say, committed adultery, or being afflicted with, say, a skin condition. Both states were stains paradoxically bleached (remediated) only by the blood of sacrifice. Absent sacrifice, the unclean person was foreclosed from ritual participation.

Other examples. A woman who just gave birth was considered unclean, as was a person who suspected of leprosy (often psoriasis). (*See* Lev. 12, 13). A man who had experienced a recent discharge was unclean, regardless of whether the discharge was continuing. The man with a seminal discharge was also unclean, but only until evening. A couple who had recently copulated was unclean, also until evening. A woman was considered unclean for the duration of her period, pegged at seven days. (Lev. 15)

A blood sacrifice would scour the unclean person. The animal used for the blood sacrifice was required to be whole: a male without blemish. Entrails and legs could be offered only after ritual washing, perhaps like the priest washing her hands in the *lavabo* prior to offering the Great Thanksgiving. (Lev. 1, 3) Only a clean person was permitted to eat the meat of sacrifice; only the clean Christian is permitted to ingest the Holy Communion. (*cf.* Lev. 7:20 *with* 1 Cor. 11:27.)

A sacrificial animal was intrinsically clean only if coming from the category of animals defined by law as clean. Not all animals were considered clean, (Lev. 11), just as some people were considered categorically unclean.

Without debating the merits of the Mosaic law, especially in the particular, suffice it to say that the purity Moses exacted from the Hebrew people distinguished them from the people living in neighboring nations.

Two millennia later, by the time of Jesus, the Pharisees had embellished upon and misconstrued the purity laws to such a degree that their constructs had become *parodies* of the original. They accused Jesus' disciples of failing to wash before eating, though not for fear of the spread of disease. They were concerned about ritual impurity before God. (*See* Mk 7:5) They extrapolated their exaggerated practice from their bastardization of the original Mosaic law.

Because washing had become more ritualistic than functional to Pharisees, the practice had lost any real meaning. Worse, the ritual had become even *more* ritualistic, if you will. The person was now required to wash himself to his elbow. He was also required to sprinkle his meal with pure water.

Modern science has discovered the dangers lurking in e-coli and other bacteria and viruses. We wash our hands functionally, not just before eating, but also after using the bathroom, after shaking hands with someone who is sick, and upon entering a hospital room, all to prevent the spread of germs.

More recently, we have learned that some germs and bacteria are necessary and helpful, and washing too often with antibacterial soap inhibits the production of healthy bacteria that serve to strengthen the human immune system.

When I was a boy, my mother would inspect our hands before supper: *Have you washed, yet?* She never asked whether I'd used soap, hot water or a clean towel. She checked only to see whether my hands were wet. I would often stick my hands under the faucet just to get them wet, in order to fool Mom, and certainly not because I was worried about getting sick. I would use soap only when Mom would stand over me to make sure I was actually *washing* my hands.

Wash the hands, fingertip to elbow, and Jesus looked incredulously at the Pharisees. *You must be kidding?* The Pharisees washed to wash, not to avoid the spread of germs. They washed because washing itself was about washing, and nothing else. Washing begets washing. Their bath was devoid of meaning. The Pharisees had no intention of cleaning under their fingernails.

Law without rationale is a waste of everybody's time, this much Jesus understood and preached regularly. Moses had prohibited the eating of pigs probably because so many people got sick eating undercooked pigs, not because the pig is a lesser creature than the cow in God's estimation. Moses founded Levitical law upon rock and not air, upon reason and not whim.

As a priest, I choose not to wash my hands ritualistically because I find no meaning in the practice. It is a waste of time at best, and antithetical to the purpose of communion at worst. Jesus eschewed empty ritual, and water flowing across my hands cleanses neither my hands nor my soul. Hence, the ritual smacks of air and not rock. I hope to signal to congregations that I don't see any reason for ritualistic washing without foundational purpose. I *have* been made clean: 2000 years ago. My cleansing is sustaining, and not in need of a repeat performance. Also, I am not comfortable standing before God and the people to declare that I am washing *my hands*, as the Psalmist writes and priests quote, *in innocence*. I may be clean, but I am anything but innocent. Hence – my desperation meets divine grace at communion. Why should I pretend otherwise?

The Pharisees rebuked Jesus because his disciples did not wash their hands before eating, but Jesus rebuked them in return. *You are way too worried about the outside, and not the inside,* he accused them. *You are setting aside the commandment of God so you can cling to human traditions.*

Jesus also took them to task for other juvenile practices. You congratulate yourselves for condemning people to death when they curse mother and father; yet you encourage people to divert their money "for God" when they ought to use their money to help their parents. It's fine if your parents live in poverty or starve, so long as the church receives its ten percent. (*See* Mk. 7:8-13)[21]

It isn't the acolyte's water and a bowl named for the ritual "*lavabo*" that cleanses the priest's soul, it is the grace of God. Grace alone infuses the heart turned heavenward.

1	Give judgment for me, O LORD, for I have lived with integrity; * I have trusted in the Lord and have not faltered.
2	Test me, O LORD, and try me; * examine my heart and my mind.
3	For your love is before my eyes; * I have walked faithfully with you.
4	I have not sat with the worthless, * nor do I consort with the deceitful.
5	I have hated the company of evildoers; * I will not sit down with the wicked.
6	I will wash my hands in innocence, O LORD, * that I may go in procession round your altar,

Psalm 26:1-6, BCP.

Claiming self-innocence like a King David (ostensibly the psalm's author) when he faced real, live enemies threatening to kill him is

---

[21] Maybe this is why Jesus' brother James admonished those holding "true religion" to remember, that true religion is evidenced by deeds, the life lived, the gifts given, the charity offered, and not mere words. (*See* James 1, 2)

one thing. Claiming self-innocence esoterically in the face of the dark sinfulness of humanity (and one's complicity in that darkness) seems antithetical to both the Gospel itself and the practice of Holy Communion. The priest's claim of innocence is duplicitous.

Jesus invited the people to listen to his explanation. What counts, he told them, is the condition of the heart, and not external ritual. External ritual cannot scour the soul. The heart is scoured by what you do, or as it is sometimes put, *what you do speaks so loud I can't hear what you say.* By the same token, being born into the right tribe or nation, the right circumstance, or the right social class, will not make you clean.

Jesus and the Woman

Following this discussion, Jesus violated the fundamental principle found in our baptismal covenant: *respect the dignity of every human being.* Jesus treated this foreign woman with disdain and disrespect.

Jesus had wandered into gentile territory, where he came upon this *Syrophoenician* woman. She was foreign to both Jesus and his cronies. (Perhaps this irony is obvious: Jesus in the woman's land was the outsider, not the woman.) Being foreign to these Jews, this woman is patently unclean. Compounding her own *uncleanness*, this woman's daughter harbors an *unclean spirit*. She asks Jesus to heal her daughter. Jesus responds by calling both of them, the woman and her daughter, dogs. Scavengers, dirty and nipping at heels, and not that cute Labrador puppy you just rescued. This woman is a wild and dirty yapping dog ready to bite you so she can steal your food.

Heal my daughter. Was she as disdainful as Jesus? Did she spit these words at him?

The children should be fed before the dogs, Jesus responded in measure.

Even the dogs eat the children's scraps; surely you can spare a scrap of grace.

Children lived at the bottom of the Jewish hierarchical heap, just above dogs. This woman accepted Jesus' metaphor and acquiesced to the traditional Jewish caste system, even though it was not *her* system. She willingly located herself beneath the Jews. She didn't care. She was tired and scared. Her daughter was sick and Jesus was her last resort. Moreover, some deep part of her must have intuited that Jesus would, in the end, be true to his own nature. Being true to himself rather than tradition and expectation, his integrity would force him to acknowledge her dignity and that of her child. He would help her daughter. By allowing herself and her child to be compared to dogs, she backed Jesus into a corner and forced him to elevate her. Sometimes you will find God fighting against you and you must back God into a corner and force God to elevate you.[22]

Throughout the centuries, Christian scholars and mystics have apologized for and even rationalized Jesus' peculiar, if not bad, response towards this woman. Jesus tested her, some have explained, to see whether her faith was real. Or, others have postulated, Jesus' insistence that the children be fed first meant that this woman and her dog-child would be fed – naturally over time. Just as Paul insisted later in his letter to the Romans, saving non-Jews had always been part of God's plan.

At least one modern scholar, Gerd Theissen[23] locates this intercourse in its cultural and political context. Rural and agricultural Galilee produced food for urban areas, and during droughts and other times of crisis, the rural agrarian people would have resented growing food for people in the cities. *Let the children eat first,* Theissen asserts, was a political statement on behalf of the agrarian workers. Consider Paul's own use of this aphorism that was undoubtedly common in the day: *do not muzzle the ox while it is treading.* (1 Tim. 5:18; 1 Cor. 9:9)

---

[22] Thank you, Robert DeWetter, for this insight. Robert is a faithful Episcopal priest serving Snowmass Chapel in Colorado.
[23] Theissen, Gerd. Gospels in Context, Fortress Press (1992). *See* p. 64.

But Jesus *isn't* picking a fight with the woman accidentally or unintentionally, no more than Jesus unintentionally spat to heal the deaf and dumb man. Spit was offensive, and Jesus spat offensively for a reason. Jesus sparred with this Syrophoenician woman offensively for a reason.

It's about the spit, stupid. It's about the epithet, stupid.

When I was in the sixth grade, a classmate of mine named David would bully me. He would call me names in front of the other kids to shame me, and he would dance around me like Mohammad Ali as if to punch me. He would sneak up behind me and pretend to spit into my hair. One time, he actually did spit into my hair, and I was humiliated.

Women spit in men's faces to retaliate against them scornfully. In movies, prisoners spit at their captors. In Scripture, spitting likewise expressed scorn. *They spit in my face,* Job said. (Job 30:10) *I did not hide my face from mocking and spitting,* Isaiah wrote on behalf of the suffering servant. (*See* Isaiah 50:6) (*cf.* Nb. 12:14, with its implication that being spat upon makes one unclean.)

Jesus predicted ahead of time that he would be spat upon in derision, and sure enough, the Roman soldiers spat on Jesus as part of the passion. (*cf.* Mk. 10:34 *with* Mk 14:65; Lk 22:63; and Matt. 27:30)

Therefore, when Jesus spat into his own hands, rubbed them together, spreading tacky spit across his fingers, and thrust these tacky fingers into the deaf man's mouth and smoothed the spit onto the man's tongue, Jesus was acting *ironically*. The man was an outsider, made so by infirmity and the fact that he was a beggar – just like the Syrophoenician woman was an outsider by her non-Jewishness. Jesus acknowledged the man's low position the same way he acknowledged the Syrophoenician woman's, by degrading him. Insulting him. Making sure it was clear to anybody watching that this man lurked at the bottom of the heap.

Did Jesus look on this man with compassion? Did he look on the Syrophoenician woman with compassion? Or were they mere dogs to Jesus?

Jesus lived in an honor-shame society. Status meant everything in Jesus' day: who was in, and who was out. Being a Roman citizen accorded you honor. If you were Jewish, you might have hung on one or two rungs lower, but being Jewish accorded you more than just a modicum of self-esteem. The Romans might have *appeared* higher, but Jews *understood themselves* to be closer to God. God esteems you as Jewish, and thank God you aren't like one of those *dogs,* the Romans, Samaritans, or other foreigners or outsiders – blind or crippled[24] or beggars. Thank God I am a man and not a woman, an adult and not a child, a master and not a servant. Thank God I'm not like that fellow over there, the one beating his chest and crying out to God, *be merciful to me, a sinner.* (Luke 18:9-14)

The Syrophoenician dog and the deaf beggar found themselves clinging to the very bottom rung, but this Syrophoenician woman had enough self-esteem, enough chutzpah, to do what any desperate person with any amount of dignity would do. She reminded Jesus that dogs eat crumbs. *I am some-body!* She forced everybody present, not just Jesus, to see her and her daughter as human, children of God both, despite the congregation's collective disdain.

Jesus had disdained both this woman and the beggar, literally and figuratively spat at them, insulted them, and appeared contemptuous – that is, until he healed them. That is, until he obliterated every socio and legal barrier blocking grace.

It wasn't until later, long *after* Jesus was crucified, raised from the dead, and the early church assembled itself in its full diversity, that Jesus' scandalous welcome of the Syrophoenician woman and the deaf man could be appreciated.

Peter fell into a trance in which he saw a sheet extend from heaven to earth. The sheet contained *all* manner of animal. Peter was hungry, and he heard a voice tell him to kill something to eat. Many of the animals on the sheet were Moses-unclean – pigs, shellfish, and the such. The obtuse Peter had not yet appreciated how Jesus' clan included all sorts and conditions, not just Jews. *All*

---

[24] "Crippled" used intentionally for its inherent element of insult.

are welcome, not just Christians. My family is those who do the will of the Father.

Where was Peter when Jesus told the scandalous story of the *good,* yet very unclean, *Samaritan* who aided the victim of crime, while otherwise *clean* people refused to do so? Or what about that time Jesus repeatedly cast out the unclean spirit, over and over and over again, *legion,* authorizing the collective legion to enter equally unclean pigs, sending them crazed across cliffs. Peter had forgotten that Jesus had healed another woman who was unclean because of her unclean issue of blood, that Jesus had healed this unclean Syrophoenician woman's daughter and this unclean deaf man.

Peter had forgotten that Jesus spat before healing some people, and slapped others in the face. Peter did not yet understand that Jesus slaps each of us, spits at every needy person, not as an insult to us, but to our infirmities. Jesus saves whoever is in need. Wake up! Wake up! It isn't the person at the bottom of the heap who needs grace. That person already possesses it. It is the person at the top who needs it, exactly because he thinks he doesn't.

True religion scandalizes and shocks and slaps you out of your prejudicial complacency. *Call nothing I have made unclean,* the voice reminded a Peter who needed reminding. Nothing I have made, and yet, good religious folks, née Christians, refer to God's creation as unclean all the time. Muslims or Jews. Gay, transgendered, or bisexual. Whites denigrating blacks, and religious casting aspersions on atheists. Undocumented aliens, a/k/a illegal immigrants. (What more revealing moniker could there be?) Poor Latinx workers deemed good enough to pick tomatoes and clean your house, but not welcome to build a life for themselves in your town. Build a wall; keep them out.

Peter and the early church could not imagine a church in which non-Jews were welcome without conversion. Their church was Jewish, a sect of faithful Judaism. Now God was extending the bounds, the Holy Spirit offered freely to non-Jews, the uncircumcised, prior to conversion.

You have torn us and now you have healed us, the prophet wrote. (Hos. 6:1, *para.*) And who knows the ways in which God accepts life as it is, acquiesces or bows to status, mocking it, and eventually obliterating it. In some sort of passive non-violent movement, Jesus acknowledged and still acknowledges human barriers, almost laughingly, perhaps satirically. *It is not right to give the children's food to the dogs. Here, let me spit on your tongue so you may be healed. Call nothing God has made unclean.* A rolling of the eyes, or – *what you do speaks so loud I cannot hear what you say* – and Jesus heals those who should not be healed, convention plus his own words notwithstanding. No need to wash those hands. No need whatsoever.

Chapter 7

Jesus Scandalously Opens the Communion Table to all

Canaanite (Syrophoenician) Woman: Matthew

Jesus left that place and went away to the district of Tyre and Sidon. Just then a Canaanite woman from that region came out and started shouting, "Have mercy on me, Lord, Son of David; my daughter is tormented by a demon." But he did not answer her at all. And his disciples came and urged him, saying, "Send her away, for she keeps shouting after us." He answered, "I was sent only to the lost sheep of the house of Israel." But she came and knelt before him, saying, "Lord, help me." He answered, "It is not fair to take the children's food and throw it to the dogs." She said, "Yes, Lord, yet even the dogs eat the crumbs that fall from their masters' table." Then Jesus answered her, "Woman, great is your faith! Let it be done for you as you wish." And her daughter was healed instantly.
Matthew 15:21-28

I am an Episcopalian. I grew-up in the Episcopal Church, but flirted with the charismatic evangelical world when I was in my early twenties. I returned to the Episcopal Church, where I have remained ever since.

In my charismatic days, I prayed in tongues. In my Episcopalian days, I lean into silence. Both prayer styles, tongues and silence, are surprisingly similar.

The essential objective of each of the two prayer practices is to empty or set aside the mind in order to make space for spirit. With space, the human spirit can connect more freely to God's spirit. This objective of unification is laudable, especially given the busy world in which most of us barely survive. Our brains are cluttered.

Praying with cluttered brains blocks spirit and makes it appear as though God is impervious. Praying both in tongues and by silence removes clutter and facilitates union with the Divine.

I'm no longer charismatic or evangelical, for theological and cultural reasons. I stopped taking the Bible literally years ago, plus I enjoy drinking beer too much to pretend God gets angry about it. When I utter "goddammit" or worse, I don't want to feel as though I've compromised myself (when I have not).

Choice of worship style and one's theological approach are more cultural than theological. Subconsciously, people select their particular religious expression in order to worship alongside people who dress like they do and/or think like they do. Generally, there is nothing wrong with this approach; it is human nature to want to be around like-minded people. (The problem arises when people *exclude* others.)

Moreover, one style of religious worship is not inherently better than the next. We Episcopalians aren't better worshippers than Presbyterians just because we use incense at the midnight service on Christmas Eve. God does not hear our vocal prayers better than she receives the silent meditation of the devout at a Quaker meeting. And though we Episcopalians may be skilled at performing liturgy, we often fail at other aspects of our faith expression, for example, educating our youth. In other words, being Episcopalian does not make us superior to those Christians of any other expression. Period. Each has its weaknesses and each has its strengths.

If you were to ask me, I would tell you that our greatest strength is the *via media*, Latin for *the middle way*. In practice, *via media* means this: because reasonable minds will differ on controversial issues (theological or otherwise), we come together not by creed or doctrine, but by worship. Reasonable minds can and will differ, and Scripture can be and is read in a multiplicity of ways. Looking past doctrine, worship is our binding.

Matthew wrote his Gospel in a decidedly Jewish manner, as discussed earlier. He identified the continuity between Jesus and his forebears, Abraham, Moses, and David. The new *ecclesia*, the church community, is the natural successor to the faith tradition. Jesus is the new Moses, and the church is the new Israel. Jesus issued new, or at least *reinterpreted,* law at the Sermon on the Mount.

I came not to do away with the law and the prophets, Jesus said on the Mountain, *but to fulfill them.* Neither heaven nor earth will pass away until the tiniest marks of the Hebrew alphabet are completed in the law and the prophets, every jot and tittle. (*See* Matt. 5:17, 18) The person who breaks the least commandment and teaches others to do the same will be considered least in the kingdom of heaven. Impossibly, your righteousness must *exceed* that of the Scribes and the Pharisees. (Matt. 5:19, 20) Take the law seriously: where it says, do not to kill, *do not so much as hate.* Do not bother coming to the altar if you haven't made peace with your brother. It isn't adultery that leads you astray, it is lust. (*See* Matt. 5)

As noted previously, aspects of Jesus' life paralleled those of Moses. Both boys were hidden from and miraculously escaped the evil efforts of paranoid rulers, Herod and Pharaoh, to kill them as babies. As grown men, both Jesus and Moses lived in the wilderness prior to launching their ministry careers. Both men were appointed by God. Both men issued law from a mountain.

Chapter 15, prior to the Healing – The Lead-up

Jesus was interested less in the strictures of the law than he was in the faith the law was intended to express. It didn't matter to Matthew's Jesus whether the outside of the person was clean; the inside counted far more. From inside the soul comes the filth of humanity, and not from the outside. (Matt. 15)

The Scribes and Pharisees accused Jesus' disciples of not washing their hands, as required. This requirement was an extrapolation of Levitical law, and not part of it.

Considering Jesus' approach over and above the literalness of his words, how might his approach help us as Christians in our own expressions of faith?

Following tradition, Episcopalians typically kneel at the confession of sin. What might happen if people stood instead? Would the confession still be valid? What if the priest failed to offer absolution? Would there be forgiveness? Is it the kneeling that counts, or the penitent heart? Is it the absolution that counts, or the words uttered by a contrite heart? Is it the form or the substance?

Moreover, who has *not* thought about matters besides confession while actually confessing? Lunch? The lawn that needs mowing? What, then? Is one still forgiven? Is one forgiven for letting one's mind stray?

The inside of the person, Jesus said, is where you will find the filth of hypocrisy and duplicity. You worry about appearance, yet you (Pharisees) steal from parents in the name of God? Stealing from parents in the name of God: talk about taking the Lord's name in vain! (*See generally*, Matt. 15)

It isn't what goes into a person that defiles him, Jesus continued, but what comes out of him, and his meaning is obvious, if technically incorrect. In fact, a person's stool contaminates, and what you eat can make you sick. But the soul is what is clean or unclean, the psyche, the spirit, and so what about the body?

Jesus spoke regularly about plants and agriculture. Every plant not planted by the Father will be uprooted. Mixing his metaphors, Jesus described these uprooted plants, the religious leaders, as blind men leading blind people. Nonetheless, these leaders are not planted by God, but are unruly weeds in need of pulling. God will take care of it.

Here, Peter demonstrated that intractable human trait, being slow to understand. *Please, Jesus, explain what you mean.* (Matt. 15:15, *para.*)

Jesus answered curtly: *You still do not get it?* Yet, how *could* the disciples understand this complex man, speaking one minute about a specific group of individuals, the Scribes and Pharisees, and in the next minute about another, the church.

The Canaanite Woman

Enter stage left, this intemperate, argumentative Canaanite (Syrophoenician) woman. She proves to be just as human as the rest of us, groping for grace she neither appreciates nor deserves, but Jesus is hawking. Her daughter has been tormented far too long. *Help me, help my daughter*, this tenacious woman presses Jesus and expects from God. *It isn't fair*, she intimates, which is true: it *isn't* fair. Any mother would appreciate the injustice. A child suffers without cause or reason, and wouldn't anyone who believes in a *good* God *expect* that God to right the wrong inflicted upon her child? Grace, but Jesus understands his mission to be that of Moses, narrowly to the lost house of Israel.

Israel *is* lost, the evidence is growing. Its leaders are concerned more about the outside of the cup than they are the inside. Worried about Caesar's taxes, and whether or not people are giving away too much of their money to support their parents and not the Temple. *You feed them*, Jesus commanded his disciples, but they not so surprisingly asked, *How?* (Matt. 14:16, 17, *para*.)

This woman wants to eat just a few crumbs of the children's bread. A few crumbs is all it will take. A few crumbs of grace enlivens the spirit of the entire loaf, just like a few crumbs of Holy Spirit provides complete access to the Divine. And so you see, this woman is *not* as lost as she appears, is not a lost child, after all. Faith and not DNA is the marker of family, and her faith marks her as a child of Abraham. She may not even know Abraham's name, but she proves herself worthy as his daughter nonetheless. She is not lost, to use Jesus' word, but found. And Jesus is moved by her faith, as he is always moved – by faith.

This story is the only recorded instance in Scripture in which Jesus loses an argument. He lost and then praised the winner, this so-called outsider. And so it is, this one vignette conveys the entire Matthean message. The promise is not limited to people who are direct descendants of Abraham because they are direct descendants of Abraham. *God is able from these stones to raise up children to Abraham.* (Matt. 3:9) The promise is for children of faith, those people whose insides have become clean regardless of their outsides, those who obey commandment not by form but by heart. Function over form, so you can go now – *that kind of faith* heals and makes whole.

Jesus as new Moses is offering hope not only to those who are blood-Israel, but to those who are faith-Israel. It is about *living* faith far more than *reciting* faith. It does not matter which church you belong to.

The creeds, particularly the Apostles' and Nicene, are treated as cornerstone to many Christian traditions, mine included. These creeds outline the basic tenets of Christian dogma. However, reciting the words of dogma is not the same as *living* the word of faith.

And, to repeat myself on a point worth repeating, the first word of the creeds is the Latin, *Credo,* which translates into *I believe.* Only it represents something more holistic, not mere mental ascent, but the soul's abasement: *I give myself to ...* as in:

I give myself to God, the Father Almighty.
I give myself to Jesus Christ, God's only Son.
I give myself to the Holy Spirit.

Or, better still:

I belong to God, the Father Almighty.
I belong to Jesus Christ, God's only Son.
I belong to the Holy Spirit.

The creeds are about the posture of the soul, rather than the postures of body or brain. Your brain's agreement with irreconcilable statements is irrelevant. What matters is this: that you acknowledge that you belong to the divine spark of the universe.

In her work, *The Spiritual Life,* Evelyn Underhill mentioned *Osuna,* a person I understand to be Francisco de Osuna, the Spanish

Franciscan of the sixteenth century.[25] Underhill is writing about the publican and the Pharisee, the "sinner" who beat his chest seeking mercy from God, and the man who thought so much of himself that he assumed he needed not God's help, but recognition. How do you open the spiritual channel, Underhill muses, if not by reality check? Osuna, she writes, offers this reality check. He claimed that God plays this little game with each of us called, *The loser wins*. In this game, the person holding the poorest cards does the best.

Dog, indeed. Crumbs under the table.

And so it is, Matthew essentially condensed his entire Gospel into this one story about a Syrophoenician woman, who turned faith away from form towards hope. Her hope is the hope of all people of goodwill, all who find themselves on the outside and not the inside, all who find faith in the form of donation rather than lineage. She was not Episcopalian. She was not Southern Baptist. She was neither Canaanite nor Syrophoenician.

She was a Woman of Faith.

Go therefore and make disciples of all nations, baptizing them in the name of the Father and of the Son and of the Holy Spirit. (Matt. 28:19, 20)

---

[25] Underhill, Evelyn, The Spiritual Life, Hodder & Stoughton, 1937, reprinted Martino Publishing. 2013, pp. 74, 75.

Chapter 8

What's in a Name?

While Jesus was teaching in the temple, he said, "How can the Scribes say that the Messiah is the son of David? David himself, by the Holy Spirit, declared, 'The Lord said to my Lord, "Sit at my right hand, until I put your enemies under your feet."'
David himself calls him Lord; so how can he be his son?" Mark 12:36, 37a

The Society of David

When I was ordained priest, I joined a club somewhat analogous to the Mayflower Society. Perhaps you have heard about the one qualification to becoming a member of the Mayflower Society. The person joining must stand in direct lineage to someone who sailed on the original Mayflower across the Atlantic Ocean.

To become an Episcopal priest, I joined *The Petrine Society* (my name for it). I stand in direct lineage to Peter. Legend has it that Peter's hands were laid upon the heads of people whose hands were laid upon heads of people whose hands were .... laid upon my head. Two thousand years of direct lineage, which initiated me not into the Mayflower Society, but into the holy order of priests. *The Petrine Society*.

Jesus was a heritage member of his own lineage society, *The Society of David*. Two of the Gospel writers, Matthew and Luke, go to great lengths to establish Jesus' direct lineage to Israel's King David, to prove that Jesus was legitimate heir to David's throne. *Son of David*.

Matthew numbers Jesus' *davidic* line at 42 generations: fourteen from Abraham to David; fourteen from David to *the* exile; and fourteen from the exile to "Christ." (Matt. 1:1-17) The significance of the number fourteen is obscure, although fourteen is two times seven. Seven is both the number of God and the number of perfection.

Luke reverses Matthew's order by presenting Jesus as *Son of God* first, and tracing Jesus' lineage backwards, not just to Abraham, but to Adam. (Lk. 3:23-38) Both Matthew and Luke treat Jesus' birth as virginal, a conception by the Holy Spirit.

Neither Mark's nor John's gospel mentions Jesus' lineage or the virginal conception. Mark, however, treats Jesus' role as *Son of David* respectfully and intentionally. Hence, all three synoptic gospels, Matthew, Mark and Luke, treat Jesus royally as David's Son. Again, *The Society of David*.

How is it possible, then, that this Son of David is simultaneously David's ancestor and his *lord*?[26] How can David be both father and servant? Jesus poses the riddle and neither receives nor offers the answer.

Religious Leaders

Each of the four Gospels treats the Jewish religious leaders as literary foils at the least, and objects of Jesus' scorn at the worst. Jesus looks at the people – Jewish in most cases – primarily with compassion. Even John, in his Gospel, uses the term "the Jews" frequently and pejoratively to mean religious leaders, and not *all Jewish people*. The Jewish religious leaders are that narrow group of misanthropes who positioned themselves squarely against Jesus and squarely blocking the peoples' access to real faith. In the

---

[26] Although I do not address it here, there is an obvious time element to the riddle. David preceded Jesus in time, yet Son of God is *eternal,* meaning Son of God existed in David's day. Or, time is not Newtonian, and Jesus as human existed at the same time as David, and vice versa. Jesus, both son and Lord, at least without time element. See, Rovelli, C., *The Order of Time*, Riverhead Books, 2017.)

synoptic Gospels, Luke vilifies the religious leaders generally, while Matthew emphasizes the Pharisees, and Mark the Scribes.

Scribe. None of the gospels describe the function or role of a Scribe, but it appears as though each local community had at least one of them. In all likelihood, a Scribe *inscribed* by keeping some sort of record, plus he would have transcribed Scripture by hand much like monks would do later throughout the middle ages. Also similar to medieval monks, Scribes likely had religious training, perhaps comparable to that of the Pharisees, lawyers, and other religious professionals of the day. Unlike most monks, however, the Gospel Scribes held positions of authority. Jesus thus treated them like he treated the other religious leaders, disdainfully, unless and until they proved themselves otherwise worthy.

These Scribes would have been familiar with Ezekiel's condemnation of religious leaders. Ezekiel called them shepherds who cared recklessly, at best, for God's people. (Ez. 34:23) According to Ezekiel, God intended to reject these religious leaders and supplant them in order to shepherd the people him/herself. God intended to shepherd the people directly.

The Scribes of Jesus' day, reading Ezekiel, might have anticipated God's judgment against religious leaders who segregated faith from people, but more likely, they supposed Ezekiel's prophecy had already been fulfilled by the Babylonian exile. Jesus, however, lamented over the people as sheep without a shepherd. (Mt. 9:36)

Mark's Sequence of Events Indicates Divine Removal of Religious Leaders

Upon entering Jerusalem, Jesus (in this sequence):

1. Ejected the money-changers from the Temple. Jesus ejected the money-changers as a living metaphor. I would like to suggest that Jesus' point was not the money that was changing hands, but rather, that religion had become business. Jesus intended to destroy the business of religion and replace it with faith. This Temple was God's, and did not belong to the religious leaders.

2. Cursed the fig tree for its lack of fruit. Jesus cursed the fig tree as a second living metaphor and as an immediate and direct follow-up to the cleansing of the Temple. The fig tree represented Israel in the Hebrew Scriptures. (See Joel 2:21-25) Thus, Jesus (or Mark, as author) linked Israel's failure to yield fruit directly to the careless and lamentable religious leadership. (Mark 11:20-25)
3. Confounded the chief priests, Scribes and elders regarding his authority. The religious leaders had interrogated Jesus, *By what authority are you [ejecting the money-changers from the Temple]?* Jesus said he would answer, but only if they would answer his question first: *What about John [the Baptist]?* he asked them. *Did the baptism of John come from heaven, or was it of human origin? Answer me.* (See Mk. 11:27-12:12). They realized that if they answered with integrity, by telling Jesus that they really think John's authority was not from God, the crowd would turn on them. They did not answer Jesus, so Jesus never answered them.
4. Told a parable about the landowner's son being killed by the tenants, who were then ejected so the landowner could give the vineyard to tenants who would be faithful. The vineyard represents God's people, and the tenants are its religious leaders. Just like Jesus returned the Temple to true faith (and the people), God intended to free the people from the binding and blinding faith of the religious leaders. God was fulfilling Ezekiel's promise to shepherd the people himself.
5. Confounded Pharisees about payments to Caesar. This little story catches the Pharisees violating the commandment against graven images. In their rush to trap Jesus, the Pharisees pulled a coin from their pocket, one with Caesar's head imprinted on it. Possessing the coin, and nothing else, was a violation of the commandment, exposing the hypocrisy of the Pharisees.
6. Answered Sadducees regarding bodily resurrection. Similarly, Jesus confounded the Sadducees, again to establish his spiritual authority over existing religious leaders.

7. Engaged in a one-on-one discussion with the one faithful Scribe who, Jesus said, is not far from the kingdom. This fellow expressed integrity and curiosity, a willingness to learn and expand his own faith. This is the type of religious leader God has been looking for. What is really important in faith, in religion, to God?

Jesus never answered their question, *By whose authority?* But this question is Mark's overarching thesis – by whose authority. He stated it differently early on in the Gospel, by inserting this rhetorical question after Jesus calmed the storm, and Mark asked, *Who is this, that even the wind and the sea obey him?* (Mk. 4:41)

Identity is Everything to Mark

Mark posed some form of this question repeatedly throughout the Gospel, either directly or implicitly. At the very center of the Gospel, Jesus asked his disciples, first: *Who do people say that I am?* And second: *Who do you say that I am?* (*See* Mk. 8) Only, Jesus is not asking the disciples, he is asking you and me, the readers (or hearers). Who do you say that I am?

No human being in all of Mark's story apprehends Jesus' identity correctly and completely, not even Peter, save one lone man at the end of the story. An *unclean* outsider, a Roman soldier, correctly named Jesus as God's son when Jesus hung from the cross and died, when the curtain in the Temple was torn in two, from top to bottom. He declared, *Truly this man was God's son.* (Mk. 15:39)

In order to understand the significance of Mark's literary point here, it helps to review how many people failed to grasp Jesus' identity, even when it should have been obvious. When Jesus was baptized, God announced to Jesus: *You are my Son, the Beloved.* (Mk. 1:11) No other person present, not even John the Baptist, heard these words, according to Mark. Everyone else present supposed Jesus to be the same as every other person who received baptism that day – the teenager standing in line in front of Jesus and the widow behind him. None of these people recognized Jesus before he was baptized, and none of them recognized Jesus after he was baptized.

Demons recognized Jesus as Son of God (but not the people). *I know who you are*, one of them spat at him. (See, *e.g.*, Mk. 1:24). Jesus would silence the demons and then eject them. Demons knew Jesus' identity – yes, but those who were healed – no.

Those healed failed to recognize Jesus, their healer, as Son of God.

Besides the centurion, Peter came the closest to identifying Jesus correctly. Jesus had just performed a miracle halfway – the only miracle he was not able to accomplish on the first try. *I see men as trees walking*, the blind man said.

This story – another living metaphor – immediately precedes Peter's declaration of Jesus as Messiah. Peter got it – but like the blind man healed halfway, he could see only in part. Men as trees walking. For, even though Peter correctly identified Jesus as Messiah, he assumed being Messiah meant the absence of suffering. But Jesus told Peter and the others that he was going to suffer. Peter remonstrated with Jesus, to which Jesus retorted, *Get thee behind me, Satan*. (Mk. 8:33) Peter got it, but only partway.

As Paul later wrote to the Corinthian church, *For now we see dimly, in part* ... (1 Cor. 13:12, *para*.)

Mark's point? It is not just that Peter could see only in part. It is that you and I, too, are blind people who see only in part. We understand, yet we do not understand. I believe, Lord, help thou my unbelief. (*See* Mark 9:24)

And perhaps this is why Jesus took Peter, along with James and John, to the top of the mountain immediately following Peter's half-truth, to drive the point home to Peter, to hear firsthand truth about Jesus from an impartial third party. The cloud consumed them, and a voice from heaven thundered, *This is my Son, the Beloved*, the exact words the Father had spoken to Jesus at baptism, when nobody but Jesus could hear. Only this time the words are addressed to the three disciples, plus you and me, and included this postscript: *Listen to him*. Meaning, don't rebuke him. Don't water down his words. Triumphant Messiah must paradoxically suffer.

And he did suffer. At the cross, when at the last, this outsider Roman centurion passed by, looked up to see Jesus, and declared, *Truly this man was God's Son*. (Mk. 15:39) This soldier, a man who had undoubtedly mocked and spat at Jesus just hours earlier, who perhaps had been the one who pressed thorns into Jesus' scalp, this man *apprehended* truth.

Returning to Jesus' interaction with the Scribes

Jesus' interlocution with the Scribes (about David's Son) occurred during the middle of what we call Holy Week, as Jesus and the broad group of religious leaders were going at it full throttle. As said, Jesus had threatened the authority of the religious leaders by ejecting the money changers from the Temple, embarrassed the Pharisees and Herodians by catching them with Roman coins in their pockets, and just confounded the Sadducees regarding the resurrection of the dead.

In the midst of all of this conflict, one lone Scribe appears, a man who is dangerously close to faith. He *tested* Jesus – not duplicitously, but sincerely – to see whether Jesus was *the real deal*. He clearly understood that heritage proves to be irrelevant in matters of faith, that it does not matter whether or not a person is a descendent of Abraham or of David. (Like John the Baptist is reported to have said, *God is able from these stones to raise up children to Abraham.* (*See* Matt. 3:9)) This Scribe understood inherently that existential faith, and that faith alone, is all that counts.

Perceiving faith, Jesus asked the man, *What commandment comes first?* The Scribe answered unambiguously and without obfuscation, euphemism, or trickery: *The Lord your God is One.* The singularity of God translated into love, he said: *love both God and your neighbor.* God, not Caesar. Don't carry those silly coins around in your pockets. Your devotion is to be as singular as is the very nature of God.

Jesus praised that Scribe. *You are not far from the kingdom,* he said, and I can think of only one or two other people who received such high praise from Jesus.

The Riddle

Later, but next in Mark's story, Jesus asked the group of Scribes the riddle: *How can they maintain that the Christ is the son of David? Again, how can a father call a son, Lord?* (Ps. 110:1)

Religious leaders by virtue of their position held sway over ordinary people, but that does not mean people were blind to their motives and obfuscations. Just like today, people in Jesus' day could tell when leaders were being disingenuous. Be wary of those Scribes who like to walk about in long robes and be greeted obsequiously in public, who like to take places of honor, yet *swallow the property of widows* and *offer lengthy prayers.* (Luke 20:46, 47, *para.*) The people would have enjoyed watching Jesus spar successfully with the Scribes.

Jesus' judgment against the religious leaders of his generation reverberates across the years as a stern warning to contemporary religious leaders. Faith cannot be inherited. Who cares whether you and your family have belonged to the same church for generations? Who cares whether you are descended from Peter? Which is better: to have crossed the ocean *on the Mayflower* as one expressing faith in the face of persecution? Or to lay passive claim to that same faith because of mere ancestry? Cross the ocean, but don't presume you have faith in God because you were born into a particular church and attend it on Sundays.

Who is this man? Is he Son of David? Is he Christ, the Lord of David? According to Mark, nobody knows who this man is, save the centurion. Even still, the people in the story clothed themselves in shredded cloths of faith. Little pieces of faith; and isn't that the same for all of us?

Perhaps we are all like the obstinate and blind religious leaders. Perhaps we are all like that one Scribe who came so very close to the Kingdom. Perhaps we are both.

The lone Scribe maintained his integrity. He asked questions as a curious student might rather than as a presumptuous leader or teacher might. Faith is always searching, always seeking, always hoping. Always changing.

Jesus never answered the riddle, and he let the Scribe's summary of the commandments stand. Jesus did not want to settle the matter of faith; he never does. He wanted instead to confound our understanding of faith. Everybody's faith. To inspire searching hearts, so we would not become people whose religion becomes transfixed. Who have answers yet care nothing about the questions.

Some traditional Christian theology makes very little sense, which I suppose is why spiritual guides resort to unappetizing words like *mystery* to explain the inexplicable. The concept of the Trinity is not intelligible. Descriptions are insufficient, as are metaphors and comparisons. The Trinity is not an egg (white, yolk, shell). Nor is the Trinity three males (I am father, son and brother, all in one.). In fact, God is not male at all. Nor female.[27] The virgin birth makes no sense, either, nor does the incarnation.

Where would Christianity be without the employment of *mystery*? The ephemeral resists description, and God shall not be named.

Mystery, yet I grow uncomfortable when people use mystery as an excuse to avoid thinking. Faith seeks understanding. Religion requires definition. I want to describe what I feel, what I perceive, what I believe. But here, you have this unexplained riddle smack in the middle of the Jesus story, and the riddle cannot be answered

---

[27] The best literary divide to help understand the Trinity is poetry, as in three persons dancing the circle of love, as represented in the ancient icon (describe/define).

without resorting to the word, *mystery*. Why, if not to reaffirm the existence of mystery?

Mark is writing *gospel*. Gospel is a type of writing – neither biography nor history, neither epistle nor poetry. Gospel literally means *Good News*, and it is three-dimensional writing intended to elicit a response from you and me as readers. Upon reading Mark, there is one and only one question left: *Who do you say that I am?*

You already *know* who this is. It is Jesus. God's Son. You hear the Father proclaim Jesus' identity at the outset, at his baptism. The heavens split, and God speaks words that only Jesus – and you – hear. From that point forward, you know this man's identity. But do you *really* know?

The miracles confirm Jesus' identity. Teachings confirm it. The confrontations with religious leaders confirm it. And when Peter at last proclaims Jesus as Messiah, you nod your head in full agreement. You have become Peter, knowing this Jesus to be the Son of God. *Very God of Very God*. Yes, this is Messiah. Only you, like Peter, *see men as trees walking*.

For when Jesus starts talking about suffering, you and I naturally join with Peter and declare that we, too, cannot believe that Jesus as Messiah would be required to suffer. Suffering is not anybody's – much less his – destiny. *I will not let you suffer*. (Moreover, if I admit that Jesus must suffer, then who's to say that I won't be required to suffer?)

Only, Jesus rebukes Peter. *Being* Messiah means *suffering*, and not instant gratification or glory. There will be no restoration of the throne of David, at least not in Israel, but how can that be? Jesus' negative tone continues throughout the rest of the Gospel, only it grows worse. My followers must carry their own crosses. Peter, you too will suffer. Rob, you too will suffer.

Despite Jesus' dark promise, you decide to climb the Mountain with Peter, James and John anyway. Steady, one foot in front of the other, you remain unsure of what awaits you at the top. Once there, you glimpse the startling sight of Jesus conferring with the law and the prophets. The heavens break open this second time, only the voice reassures you. *This is my Son; listen to him.* Take him seriously when he speaks to you about suffering.

Suffering, despite the fact that Jesus appears to be traveling to Jerusalem to reign as Son of David. You remain loyal, joining the crowds shouting, *Hosanna,* and throwing palm branches along the road. Jesus rides the road regally on the back of the colt. Next, Jesus *acts* Messiah-like by reclaiming the Temple from its corrupt occupation.

All of this is well and good – for you *know* this man to be God's Son. You've been able to distance yourself emotionally from the promise of suffering – that is, until the end of the upcoming week, when Jesus is crucified.

You were there all along, you've known all along about the roped connection between this man and God. This rope cannot be severable, but there are those final dark words, *My God, My God, why have you deserted me?* (Mark 15:34, Jer.) Messiah suffer? It is finished, and Jesus suffers just as he predicted.

The Lord said to my Lord,
Sit at my right hand
and I will put your enemies
under your feet.

Along comes this centurion who speaks like the lone voice of a Greek tragedy, a no-person who has no buy-in because he is neither Jewish nor faithful. He correctly identifies Jesus: *Surely this man was God's Son.*

You thought you understood, but you didn't. This outsider alone understands the truth, that which Jesus alluded to long before, with the little riddle, *The Lord said to my Lord ... how can that be?*

Both Man and God, Jesus is both Son of David (man) and Son of God (God). Jesus answered his own riddle, not with words, but by his life.

For the Son of Man came not to be served, but to serve, and to give His life a ransom for many. (Mk. 10:45) Jesus said this to all those following, you and me included.

Jesus condemned the Scribes because they were obstinate and blind, but not everyone lacked faith. There was one pure soul, a woman. Immediately after posing the riddle, at the end of the long sequence of stories directed against the religious leaders, Jesus sat down opposite the Temple treasury to watch people donate their money.

The rich donated a great deal of money, but this one tired old woman, a hunched widow, dropped two pennies into the basket, all she had to live on. Sacrifice. This woman *believed,* lived a faith that insisted God is in charge, God loves her, and God will care for her. She trusted.

So there you have it. The curious Scribe and this widow were the two people nearest the kingdom. Plus the Roman centurion. And I suppose that is the irony. The one who questions with a desire to learn has faith. The one who possesses nothing has everything; and the one standing outside is the one inside.

Who do you say that I am?

Chapter 9

The Goo That is Faith

Jairus and the Woman with the Hemorrhage

Now when Jesus returned, the crowd welcomed him, for they were all waiting for him. Just then there came a man named Jairus, a leader of the synagogue. He fell at Jesus' feet and begged him to come to his house, for he had an only daughter, about twelve years old, who was dying. As he went, the crowds pressed in on him. Now there was a woman who had been suffering from hemorrhages for twelve years; and though she had spent all she had on physicians, no one could cure her. She came up behind him and touched the fringe of his clothes, and immediately her hemorrhage stopped. Then Jesus asked, "Who touched me?" When all denied it, Peter said, "Master, the crowds surround you and press in on you." But Jesus said, "Someone touched me; for I noticed that power had gone out from me." When the woman saw that she could not remain hidden, she came trembling; and falling down before him, she declared in the presence of all the people why she had touched him, and how she had been immediately healed. He said to her, "Daughter, your faith has made you well; go in peace." While he was still speaking, someone came from the leader's house to say, "Your daughter is dead; do not trouble the teacher any longer." When Jesus heard this, he replied, "Do not fear. Only believe, and she will be saved." When he came to the house, he did not allow anyone to enter with him, except Peter, John, and James, and the child's father and mother. They were all weeping and wailing for her; but he said, "Do not weep; for she is not dead but sleeping." And they laughed at him, knowing that she was dead. But he took her by the hand and called out, "Child, get up!" Her spirit returned, and she got up at once. Then he directed them to give her something to eat. Her parents were astounded; but he ordered them to tell no one what had happened. Luke 8:40-56. (*See also Matt. 9:18-26, Mk. 5:21-43*)

Faith

The writer to the Hebrews describes faith as substance. (Heb. 11:1). When I think of faith as substance, I think of the green goo I used to put in my kids' Christmas stockings when they were eight years old: malleable, sticky, gooey, substance. Faith. Substance, by definition, must be *substantial,* even though invisible, like the elemental building blocks of the physical universe (its *substantiality*): atoms and molecules. Substance as the goo that constitutes the primary structure of the universe.

Faith is substance, Hebrews continues, bounded by hope. Hope encases faith, like a shell encases a nut. There can be no faith without hope.

Emil Brunner writes[28] that we, as human beings, live in three dimensions simultaneously, the past, the present and the future. Faith to Brunner addresses the past by referring to the historical event of Jesus Christ. Brunner also writes of faith in both the present and the future, conflating time while attempting to retain the distinctions of time.

I find Brunner's schematic confusing. Faith must be time-oriented. Start with hope as the primary element of faith (*substance of things hoped for*). Hope by necessity points to the future and not the past. How can faith that is constituted by hope point backwards in time? History cannot be an element of faith because it is past, done. Faith must be alive in the present, directing one's attention to the future. Again, faith must be time-oriented. In other words, the acceptance of, acquiescence to, or intellectual agreement with the historical event of Jesus Christ is not faith.

Although hope encases faith, faith is more than hope standing alone. The writer continues: Faith is evidence. It is evidence or proof that one cannot see, the proof of satisfaction or fulfillment of one's hope.

---

[28] Brunner, Emil, *Faith, Hope, and Love,* The Westminster Press, 1956.

The phrase, *substantial evidence,* comes to mind – tangible, like a talisman of things that one would otherwise not see, things that would otherwise be incapable of apprehension, like a ghost, the wind or a black hole. The proof of a ghost is experienced by extraneous and impossible sounds at night, or in the unprovoked movement of a letter from one side of the desk to the other. The proof of a black hole is the disappearance of stars. Faith is proof of a God and grace unseen, yet the deeds of which are extant. (As Paul writes, one need look only into the heavens to find proof of God. *See* Rom. 1)

Consisting thus of substance and proof, faith is nonetheless invisible, and too often unknown. Even people who possess faith cannot readily explain its nature, although they *know it when they see it,* as the Supreme Court quip goes. Faith is far more than one's opinion about religion or the thought processes one engages in order to conclude that a creed is factually accurate.

To repeat myself, physicists believe multiple dimensions, or universes, exist simultaneously side-by-side. According to speculation by contemporary physicists, it is possible and even likely that matter from one dimension transmits into another dimension – perhaps not easily, but a little like air flowing through a screen door.

I tend to think of the location of heaven not according to the arcane notion of existing above the chasm, but right here, in the dimension next door, just a hair's breadth away.

What then does it mean to have faith?

Catholics treat works as a necessary ingredient to salvation. Eternal bliss hinges upon one's works, the good one accomplishes in life. Indeed, Scripture addresses works regularly, the prophets constantly excoriating Israel or Judah for their failure to care for others. James, the brother of Jesus, wrote plainly, *faith without works is … dead.* (James 2:26) Jesus took people to task for not acting on behalf of others. Consider the story of the *Good Samaritan,* which is all about works. (Luke 10:25-37)

Protestants treat faith as the opposite, that faith alone is necessary for salvation. *For by grace you have been saved through faith* ... (Eph. 2:9). Paul wrote elsewhere that justification before God comes through faith (Rom. 5:1), and faith consists of *believing in your heart that Jesus is Lord and confessing with your mouth that God raised him from the dead* (Rom. 10:9, *para.*) – then you will be "saved." Faith to Protestants naturally begets good works.

Only, as my New Testament seminary professor taught,[29] Paul is ambiguous with regard to whose faith is required. Yours, or Jesus'?

Jesus the Christ died on the cross, not you. Jesus the Christ rose from the dead, not you.

A salvation by grace requiring a person to act in order to be saved, even as evidence of salvation, seems paradoxically impossible. Moreover, the twin acts of "believing" and "confessing" are exactly that, *acts.* The minute you believe, your belief becomes work. The minute you respond, your response becomes work. To the extent that your salvation depends upon either or both of these two actions, your salvation is inherently one of work. You must own them – which brings into question personal salvation by intellectual belief as, like I said, paradoxically impossible, or perhaps oxymoronic.

On the other hand, it is said that you can do absolutely nothing to earn or deserve salvation, including believe. Belief itself is a gift, even when it is a gift that elicits a response. What, then, is "belief?"

Credo, I believe, being less the intentional choice to believe and more the posture of the soul, it is like yoga. One *leans* oneself into the Other. You donate yourself to, you yield to faith and a life and a God who is so much larger than you are. And even your ability to do that – to lean – is a gift from God.

Whose faith? Your faith or Jesus' faith? Paul's ambiguity lends itself to the mystery of communion. The life and walk of faith is a joint venture. You are *invited* like Adam and Eve to walk alongside God through the garden in the cool of the day ...

---

[29] The Rev. Christopher Bryan, Ph.D., D.D.

Faith. Substance of things hoped for, evidence of things not seen. Substance, goo, some elemental foundation of the universe, invisible yet nonetheless extant. Substance that equals hope. Imbibes hope. Imbues hope.

Your hope, God's hope, the hope of the universe and the hope of those you love. Hope, which means you desire something at parchment level. No mere desire, your hope is tinged with this atom-sized hint or suspicion that what you feel is solid, has foundation, is not vanity, that God is on your side, that when you, with this mustard seed inclination of yours, say to Mt. McKinley, *Be taken up and cast into the sea*, you suppose that casting into the sea and sinking to the bottom of the ocean are exactly what God intends and will accomplish.

Jairus and the Woman with the Hemorrhage

Following is an ordered list of stories found in Luke around the miracle of Jairus' daughter:

- Jesus calmed the storm
- Jesus cast out the Gerasene demoniac
- Jairus asked Jesus to heal his daughter
  On the way to heal the girl, the woman
  with the hemorrhage/issue of blood
  touched Jesus' cloak (outer garment)
- Jairus' daughter was raised to life from the dead

Imagine yourself to be the woman with the 18-year hemorrhage. You have begged God to deliver you from your affliction, without result. Literally begged, you've tried bargaining, cajoling, even threatening God, but God has remained silent. You've even cried out to other gods and prayed for resolution – any resolution, perhaps even death – but nothing.

One day, you hear that some *Master* is passing through town. For some strange reason, the honorific itself, *Master*, ignites in you latent desire and faith, hope and belief. Elemental concrete, and you wonder whether you audibly heard the word or just imagined it: *Now*. Now you *must* yield to the spark, now you *must* reach out against every modern-day convention and now you *must* touch the clothing of a man – a *man* (against convention and law) – and that being a man you do not even know. You have *hope*, but yours is not merely a hollow wish, it is a living hope that removes mountains to the sea, stakes claim to reality change. The curve of light is straightening.

Faith. If hope is the foundational element to faith, then fear is the foundational element to doubt. The disciples were afraid when the gale spumed waves across the bow of the boat and threatened to drown them. The disciples shook Jesus awake - *Don't you care?*

"*Don't you care*": the three words uttered most often when one is afraid. Faith being the antithesis to fear, blessed assurance, the promise that God *does* care, will act on *your* behalf. When you give yourself over to God without force, when you *lean into God*, you see that God *is* on your side, with you, never to leave nor forsake you. That *those who come to God obtain the realization that God honors seekers* ... (Heb. 11:6, *para.*)

God is good.
All the time.
All the time.
God is good.

God cares not abstractly for the world but concretely for you. Intimate God designs good things for those who hope, for those who lend themselves to the incredulity of belief, for those who let go of the sense that God is angry and does not care. That God is remote. Let God into your soul as a smoldering ember of hope and watch the storms act like trees felled, with just two simple words: *Be still*.

Be still, and that same Jesus who loved his friends completely, rebuked with divine guardianship the wind and waves for threatening Jesus' friends.

Jesus' faith, yet he was incredulous at his friends' fear: *How can it be that you have no faith?* (Mk 4:40, *para.*) I am right beside you, and even though your faith may be inadequate, mine is not. Submerge yourself into my faith. Let yourself *become* part of my faith.

In the very next story, the Gerasene man full of "demons" was so incapacitated that he was completely incapable of possessing faith. He was mentally incapacitated and unable to conjure any machinations whatsoever, least of all faith. Only, Jesus had enough faith for the both of them, so he ordered the man's twisted thought patterns untangled, commanded his jailers to flee. Tangible evil, they flew ironically into *unclean* pigs that, in turn, ran themselves off a cliff. Jesus' sole instruction to the man once he could think clearly was to tell others. Tell them:

God is good.
All the time.
All the time.
God is good.

All one needs to bring to God is the *hope* that God cares. That *hope* will enable you to yield, to steer into safe harbor. *All shall be well, and all shall be well, and all manner of things shall be well.*[30] It will be good with your soul. God exists, and God rewards. God is good, even to those people lacking the ability to muster faith on their own, especially to those people lacking the ability to muster faith on their own, the disciples included.

And if you already have faith, remember this: faith is paradoxical. Can it be said that faith is yours? That faith belongs to you, that you *have* – own or possess – faith? If it emanates from God, then you can do nothing but offer thanks.

Jairus and the Woman: Faith

The synagogue official, Jairus, approached Jesus, fell at his feet, and begged Jesus to heal his daughter. (Lk. 8:41) The girl was terribly sick and about to die. While Jesus made his way to the girl, she died.

---

[30] Julian of Norwich.

(Lk. 8:49) Perhaps she died because Jesus stopped to speak with the woman who was bleeding. (See Lk. 8:43-48)

People pressed in on Jesus from all sides. Even though this *multitude* had gathered about Jesus, he felt power escape.

Who touched me? He asked.

The disciples were incredulous. *You see the multitude pressing in on you. How can you ask that question?* Are you serious?

Jesus *was* serious. Despite the crowd pressing in on him, people wanting a piece of him, he felt the electric tinge of hope elemental to faith. This daughter of Israel had been sick for eighteen years. Worse, she had been *unclean* for eighteen years. (*See* Lev. 15:25) Her impurity was contagious, according to the law, and anyone who touched what she had touched became unclean. Unclean, disconnected from temple ritual and other people. Unclean, like the pigs into which Jesus cast the equally unclean demons. Unclean, like the very land on which the man who had the demons lived (for it was foreign land). Unclean, this woman was an untouchable. She wasn't allowed to come near others, all because her body would not stop bleeding. Eighteen years. No human contact until she had the audacity to graze a finger against Jesus' cloak.

Undoubtedly she lacked nutrients, particularly iron, having lost so much blood. She would have been lethargic and unengaged, even depressed. Yet, something tugged at her so deeply, some hope rooted in possibility. She must have believed, or hoped, after eighteen years of wrestling, that God is good; all the time; all the time; God is good.

As Jesus approached, she gathered all her depressed strength together and pushed herself through a crowd that was already pressing hard against Jesus, and despite every law forbidding her from doing so, she reached out and touched Jesus' clothes. Shocked, not that an unclean woman touched him, but that someone actually had enough spring-water hope to elicit his faith. Scandalized at her hope, Jesus turned around. *Who touched me?* A question that was not so much accusation as promise.

What do you mean, "Who touched me?" His disciples asked.

The power, I felt it leave me. Jesus redoubled.

The woman was by now trembling with the fear of God and confessed openly at Jesus' feet: *I touched you. I touched you thinking to myself that if I just touch this little piece of you … if only … I know it is wrong, I know I'm unclean. But you see, I've had this blood hemorrhage for eighteen years. It's kept me from having children. My husband left me. My village shuns me. I have only one shard possession remaining – hope. And even that, they tell me, is not good enough. I do not go to synagogue or Temple. How can I go when they won't let me anywhere near? So I touched you* … she trembles again, tears slipping onto her cheek, her chin, the ground … *only when I touched you, what can I say? How can I tell you? I'm alive. Again alive.*

Daughter, Jesus said simply – not Daughter of Abraham or Daughter of Israel, just *Daughter – your faith has made you well. Go in peace, and be healed.* You are whole. Complete. No longer untouchable, *not that you ever were.*

God has taken your side, and I don't know whether Jesus' question – *Who touched me?* – was ironic or not. It seems to be, but so does his later statement, as he continued moving away from this woman and on to Jairus' house, where people were wailing and gnashing their teeth over the death of Jairus' daughter. *She has died,* they told Jairus while he and Jesus were still on their way; *trouble the Master no more.*

Indeed, this daughter had died, but Jesus shook his head in rebuttal: *No, she is asleep.* The testimony of the entire household told the man that his daughter was dead, but Jesus testified otherwise. He saw things differently, just like he sees things differently from you and me. He saw and sees through eyes we don't possess. Jesus is Superman with x-ray vision, and he sees through obfuscation and falsehood. The girl was asleep. *Do not be afraid any longer, only believe.*

Which is the same imperative as, *Be not afraid, believe.* Hope and believe, and fear not death nor tempest nor storm that threatens.

She is asleep, as though there exists some hidden, unseen world located below or perhaps above the *substantial* matter that appears to be earth. You see the earth and the rocks and the sky and people's flesh and animals' fur. You see birds flying and trees budding, but do you *really* see? Open your eyes to reality, not the physical sub-reality. This physical world moves according to the spiritual world, and not the other way around.

Forty-plus dimensions, and Jairus' daughter has slipped quietly into the dimension next door. She is not dead, she is asleep. (Lk. 8:52) Neither you nor I are dead, we are asleep.

What do you hope for? Not just desire or want, as in, I want to win the lottery. I want to travel to Ireland. And certainly not, what do you covet?

Rather, what golden thread of hope is woven through the fabric of your soul? Tiny bits of gold glitter that, should you apprehend with faith, might change your entire world? Save people? Right the wrongs of the universe? Hope, something substantial above and beyond vague desire, yet concrete and deeply imbedded in the soul. That deep and desperate hope of Jairus. Of the woman with the hemorrhage.

Neither was afraid even in the face of the stark cruelty of fear. They combatted fear with the twin gifts of God: hope and faith.

Jesus commanded the little girl, *Talitha, kum.* Little girl, I say to you, arise! Return, O soul, from the world next door, flow like air through the screen door. Her soul returned, igniting molecules and cells and DNA, and she arose.

She is but asleep. And the irony is this: faith is seeing. It is seeing things as they are, not as they appear to be. Looking at the world through the eyes of God. Substantially, there is far more to this world than atoms and molecules and cells.

Chapter 10

Would the Real Prodigal Please Stand Up?

Prodigal Son I

[11] Then Jesus said, "There was a man who had two sons. [12] The younger of them said to his father, 'Father, give me the share of the property that will belong to me.' So he divided his property between them. [13] A few days later the younger son gathered all he had and traveled to a distant country, and there he squandered his property in dissolute living. [14] When he had spent everything, a severe famine took place throughout that country, and he began to be in need. [15] So he went and hired himself out to one of the citizens of that country, who sent him to his fields to feed the pigs. [16] He would gladly have filled himself with the pods that the pigs were eating; and no one gave him anything. [17] But when he came to himself he said, 'How many of my father's hired hands have bread enough and to spare, but here I am dying of hunger! [18] I will get up and go to my father, and I will say to him, "Father, I have sinned against heaven and before you; [19] I am no longer worthy to be called your son; treat me like one of your hired hands."' [20] So he set off and went to his father. But while he was still far off, his father saw him and was filled with compassion; he ran and put his arms around him and kissed him. [21] Then the son said to him, 'Father, I have sinned against heaven and before you; I am no longer worthy to be called your son.' [22] But the father said to his slaves, 'Quickly, bring out a robe—the best one—and put it on him; put a ring on his finger and sandals on his feet. [23] And get the fatted calf and kill it, and let us eat and celebrate; [24] for this son of mine was dead and is alive again; he was lost and is found!' And they began to celebrate.

[25] "Now his elder son was in the field; and when he came and approached the house, he heard music and dancing. [26] He called one of the slaves and asked what was going on. [27] He replied, 'Your brother has come, and your father has killed the fatted calf, because he has got him back safe and

sound.' ²⁸ Then he became angry and refused to go in. His father came out and began to plead with him. ²⁹ But he answered his father, 'Listen! For all these years I have been working like a slave for you, and I have never disobeyed your command; yet you have never given me even a young goat so that I might celebrate with my friends. ³⁰ But when this son of yours came back, who has devoured your property with prostitutes, you killed the fatted calf for him!' ³¹ Then the father said to him, 'Son, you are always with me, and all that is mine is yours. ³² But we had to celebrate and rejoice, because this brother of yours was dead and has come to life; he was lost and has been found.'" Luke 15:11-32

Both sons were grown men, but they maintained infantile relationships with their father. Each believed that the father kept tally, that he related to each of them based upon their behavior, what each son did or failed to do, the good work or life each led. The father did not keep tally. The father based his relationship with each son upon the son's existential self. The fact that each was a son. Period.

The father split his estate into two, one share for each son. The younger son asked for his share prematurely, to which the father acquiesced, naturally leaving the residual estate predestined for the older son. The younger son left home. The older son stayed home to help his dad run the remaining estate – which, of course, was his. *All I have is yours,* his father had to remind him later.

This dutiful fellow may have *owned* the remaining estate, but he acted as though he did not understand this fact, that he was working his own estate. Instead, he lived his life not as owner, but as he *supposed* his father expected him to live it, doing what he assumed would be acceptable to his father.

Such a behavior pattern is borne of projection. He assumed his father expected him to act in a way he, were he a father, would expect his own son to act. He complied, you see, with his own imagination. As far as we know, this son never actually asked his father what he wanted of him. He followed his own skewed, internal compass.

Had he *really* wanted to please his father, the older son should have asked his father to tell him what that might be.

Perhaps I am wrong. Perhaps we should take the parable at face value, that the older son was faithfully dutiful to what the father wanted and expected. That the father had taught his son the difference between right and wrong, between responsibility and irresponsibility? That this elder son became the *responsible* child, putting his faith in a work ethic that so obviously eluded his younger brother.

Even still, whether by projection or growing faithfully into a responsible life, this older son's identity seems to have become so suffused with that of his father that he became unable to extricate himself to the point of self-actualization. His identity existed through his father's.

Some children follow in their parents' footsteps naturally. I think here of the daughter who goes to law school to join her father's law practice, *Smith & Smith, Attorneys at Law,* or of the family business passed down through several generations, each successive generation building successfully upon the work of the one that preceded it. Talents, traits, gifts, mark each person as uniquely qualified to continue something her parent left behind.

Perhaps this older son falls into this category. Maybe he is a natural rancher (so to speak), understands intuitively how to raise cattle and manage servants. But what if, despite his wish to follow in his father's footsteps, he is incapable of doing so? What if this son cannot ride a horse or rustle cattle and has absolutely no penchant for the great outdoors? What if he has stayed home with his father because he was afraid to leave? Resentment drips from the boy's lips upon his brother's return, suggesting dysfunction of some sort.

I wonder, was the older son stunted in his emotional growth? Had he lived his father's dream, rather than his own? If this is the case, whose fault was it? His, or his father's? (The mother is not in the picture.) Had his father left the boy enough tether to develop into an emotionally individuated man?

Turning to the younger son, suppose this boy left for psychologically fit reasons? Maybe he needed to extricate himself from his father's overshadowing presence? When I was a young adult, it became very important for me to extricate myself from both of my parents. Extrication was an essential part of my growing into my adult self.

Young children naturally learn to heed the voices of their parents, but one of the most critical movements from childhood into adulthood is emotional independence. Leave the nest, and doesn't there come a time when every person, in order to become a healthy adult, must begin to live by his own compass? *When I became a man, I put away childish things,* Paul wrote for good reason. (1 Cor. 13:11, KJV)

A parent's job is to protect the child from harm, but equally to let go – a little more each day. In contradistinction, the child's job is to push away from her parents, a little more each day. This symphonic process intensifies as the child moves into the teenage years. He pushes harder. The temptation to the parent is to clamp down, but clamping down only makes the child push harder still. The parent's first job is to respect this growing independence. While keeping the teenager safe, the parent teaches her to resist *respectfully*.

I somehow doubt – don't you? – that the younger brother broke away from his father for emotionally healthy reasons, for otherwise he would not have found himself mired in dissolute living, debauchery, and eating food that no human should consume. He had dodged responsibility by running away from home, but poverty forced him to return to the responsibility he had dodged. Perhaps he *did* need to break from his father, but not in such an unhealthy way.

But this boy *found* himself. He discovered the (beginning to the) answer to that elusive question St. Francis is said to have posed daily: *Who art thou, O God, and who am I?* Nestled among *unclean* pigs and their slop, this younger brother came to his senses. Came alive. Discovered the unholy truth about himself.

Meanwhile, the older brother did not find himself. He grew ever more resentful and incapable of articulating why. Did he mean to say, *I resent you, younger brother, because I so want to be you? You got to leave, but I had to stay. I felt bound to our Father psychologically and hate that you did not feel so bound. You escaped and I never could. It just isn't fair.*

In fact, Jesus' parable presents an older son who never disengaged psychologically from his father. He had lived a *good life,* but it was not *his* life, not one of his own choosing. His father chose this life for him. The boy became naturally resentful. Worse, he may have actually believed that obeying his father (his father's implicit demands) was the same thing as *honoring* his father. Honoring his father, but this father did not care enough to cast him a second glance, never even threw a party for him. *I have slaved for you and never once disobeyed your orders, yet you never offered me so much as a kid for me to celebrate with my friends. But, for this son of yours, when he comes back after swallowing up your property – he and his women – you kill the calf we had been fattening.* (Lk 15:29-31, Jer.) The older son could find worth – and that, hollow – only by comparing himself to his brother.

Resentment covers this man's beard like hoar on frost, only in actuality, he resented his brother less than he did his father. Passively aggressive, for deep down, he believed his father had held him prisoner passively while liberating his brother. This son was chained from the top of his head to the bottom of his feet, while his brother lived completely and scandalously unencumbered. (Or, did he?)

So many adults are emotionally stunted because they never extricated themselves emotionally from their parents. And who could blame a person for resenting the parent, regardless of the parent's actual culpability. Projected fault.

But the so-called prodigal seems afraid of his father. He knew his father to be a hard man, exacting a moral standard he could not meet. (*cf.* Matt. 25:24, the servant burying his talent did so because he *knew* the master to be harsh. Was the master actually harsh or just apparently harsh?) The father passively required obeisance to his *coda*, if you will, a type of parental legalism. The *coda* stunted both boys' growth, but this younger son freed himself by leaving, ostensibly so he could become himself, live his dream, realize himself. Only the promise of liberty proved to be elusive – liberty imprisoned the boy rather than liberate him. Life did not go as planned, and separation from his family, at least on his terms, proved to be a bad choice, life under the belly.

But now it had become clear to the boy. For the first time in months, or years, he could see. He had a plan. I will apologize and offer to work for my living. *I have sinned against heaven and against you; I no longer deserve to be called your son; treat me as one of your paid servants."* (Lk 15:19, 20, Jer.) He planned and probably practiced this surrender. Yet even while he spoke, his father waved his hands frantically and joyously welcoming the boy home. And now, this young man realizes, he has misunderstood his father all along – he still misunderstands his father.

I think of Episcopalians, of which I am one, with our so-called Prayer of Humble Access. Yes, there are times in life when each of us needs to approach God with deep contrition, with an acknowledgement of our own imperfection, incompletion, of a life somehow warped by selfishness and yes, even debauchery. Confession is cathartic and cleanses the soul.[31]

Humility is honest self-appraisal and includes the good with the bad. Recall the two men in Temple standing before God? The one man beats his chest and seeks God's forgiveness, while the other fellow points at the first, and says, *Thank you God that I'm not like that sinner over there*. Humility means coming to terms with who you really are, not who you've pretended to be all these years. Not falsely, with a false sense of incalculable worthlessness, but just

---

[31] Humility is not self-abasement, but honest self-appraisal – seeing oneself as one truly is, good and bad. The younger son *became humble* – he woke-up, came to his senses, had a self-epiphany, and *saw* that his version of the so-called life of liberty meant living lower than pigs. *I am not worthy so much as to gather up the crumbs under thy table …*

the same, not a false sense of entitlement, either. This son came to terms with his true self as he was, among the pigs.

Yet, he failed to appreciate who he was in relation to his father. He was a son. He was always a son. Even among pigs, he was a son. Returning home, he feigned servant-hood, but his father saw him and greeted him as he always was, a son. Put a son's robe on him. Slaughtered the fatted calf for this son of mine. Throw my son a party. For this son of mine was lost, but now he is home. This father – who perhaps failed to appreciate the needs of his older son to become individuated, nonetheless fully understood the nature of fatherhood. Each boy was his son, something neither son until now understood.

Christians have built churches around a theology that elevates one son over the other, the older above the younger, or the younger above the older. For example, Seventh Day Adventists, Jehovah's Witnesses, and evangelicals treat law as faith as law. You are Christian only if you stay home and tend the farm and manage the servants. You are Christian only when you live right, do the right thing. Perhaps these Christians conflate the two sons into one – you can enjoy a time of debauchery, but not *while* you are a person of faith.

Only the older son was just as legalistic and miserable as the younger son, and worse, he never became self-individuated. He never truly understood what it meant to be a son.

Other denominations have built their faith upon the doctrine of repentance. We are all the first son until that moment when we approach the father with words of self-denunciation, *I have sinned against heaven and against you …* Only, the father is not interested in words, or even that the son appears to have come to his senses. The father is interested only in his sons – both of them – as sons.

A father is always a father. He views himself as a person in relationship, only not relationship built upon the hard work of the older son, in his case, or by the repentance of the second son, in his case. Relationship by fatherhood, not by behavior. Each son was the father's son. The older son was entitled to the fatted calf anytime he wanted it (just as the younger son was entitled to take his half of the inheritance when he wanted it). The younger son – despite his scandalous lifestyle – was a son nonetheless, both when united to his father, and when separated from his father.

A relationship, you see, is a relationship, and it is not altered by your failure to understand or to grow into your adult relationship with God. Whether you find yourself legalistically faithful, or whether you find yourself scandalously alone, God is nonetheless a father to you. The status of your relationship is unaffected. You are a child of God, you always have been, and you always will be.

Not, *I believe in God the Father Almighty*, but, *I belong to God the Father Almighty*.

The irony, if not obvious, is that neither son understood the father, yet both sons remained sons throughout the entire story.

Chapter 11

Jesus as Prodigal

The Prodigal Son II

[11] Then Jesus said, "There was a man who had two sons. [12] The younger of them said to his father, 'Father, give me the share of the property that will belong to me.' So he divided his property between them. [13] A few days later the younger son gathered all he had and traveled to a distant country, and there he squandered his property in dissolute living. [14] When he had spent everything, a severe famine took place throughout that country, and he began to be in need. [15] So he went and hired himself out to one of the citizens of that country, who sent him to his fields to feed the pigs. [16] He would gladly have filled himself with the pods that the pigs were eating; and no one gave him anything. [17] But when he came to himself he said, 'How many of my father's hired hands have bread enough and to spare, but here I am dying of hunger! [18] I will get up and go to my father, and I will say to him, "Father, I have sinned against heaven and before you; [19] I am no longer worthy to be called your son; treat me like one of your hired hands."' [20] So he set off and went to his father. But while he was still far off, his father saw him and was filled with compassion; he ran and put his arms around him and kissed him. [21] Then the son said to him, 'Father, I have sinned against heaven and before you; I am no longer worthy to be called your son.' [22] But the father said to his slaves, 'Quickly, bring out a robe—the best one—and put it on him; put a ring on his finger and sandals on his feet. [23] And get the fatted calf and kill it, and let us eat and celebrate; [24] for this son of mine was dead and is alive again; he was lost and is found!' And they began to celebrate.

[25] "Now his elder son was in the field; and when he came and approached the house, he heard music and dancing. [26] He called one of the slaves and asked what was going on. [27] He replied, 'Your brother has come, and your father has killed the fatted calf, because he has got him back safe and

sound.' ²⁸ Then he became angry and refused to go in. His father came out and began to plead with him. ²⁹ But he answered his father, 'Listen! For all these years I have been working like a slave for you, and I have never disobeyed your command; yet you have never given me even a young goat so that I might celebrate with my friends. ³⁰ But when this son of yours came back, who has devoured your property with prostitutes, you killed the fatted calf for him!' ³¹ Then the father said to him, 'Son, you are always with me, and all that is mine is yours. ³² But we had to celebrate and rejoice, because this brother of yours was dead and has come to life; he was lost and has been found.'" Luke 15:11-32.

What if the "Prodigal Son" is more allegory than metaphor? That Jesus is the prodigal telling the story about himself as son of God who finds himself living in a foreign land where he does not belong?[32]

The religious leaders had just accused Jesus of consorting with tax collectors and sinners. Jesus answered them with three parables, in this order: the parable of the lost sheep, the parable of the lost coin, and the parable of the prodigal son. (*See generally*, Lk. 15)

The banal interpretation of the first two parables is probably accurate, that a typical person would search high and low for something that is both valuable and lost. The banal interpretation of the parable of the lost sheep, however, leaves one with this haunting and secondary question unanswered: Why would *any* shepherd abandon ninety-nine sheep to search for one?

When my children were young and would lose something important to them, they would become anxious. I would tell them, *Don't worry. It will show up. Lost items always show up.* Worrying never helps, and over-searching as often as not will frustrate you.

But lost people are not missing coins. Jesus ignored the haunting question in favor of the obvious point he wanted to make. Each person is of value to God, to the point of risking the security of the

---

[32] I believe Henri Nouwen explored this concept in his book, The Return of the Prodigal Son: A Story of Homecoming, Image Books/Doubleday, 1994 (reissue).

whole (in the case of the lost sheep, the whole flock). God will not abandon you, period, no matter how far you have strayed. Moreover, this God refuses to wait for the ordinary course of time to resolve lost states, but *will* search high and low for each and every one of us when we've gone missing. God is not passive but aggressive in the business of restoration.

Jesus next told the third parable, that of the prodigal son, in direct response to the religious leaders' accusations that he consorted unfavorably. As you consider whether Jesus might, in fact, be the prodigal, compare and contrast the parable itself with our understanding of the situation.[33]

First, Jesus hung with sinners, just like the younger son, the so-called *prodigal,* cavorted with sinners, those unsavory *bad* people that *good* people typically reject out-of-hand. Does God reject unsavory people? Until now, they assumed so. Lost, not found. Still lost. If Jesus were *godly* he wouldn't cavort with such people, presume the religious leaders. He would stay home religiously minding the ranch.

Second, the older son spoke in the shrill voice of the religious leaders: *This son of yours ....,* he accused both father and son. After all, your reprobate younger son has been hanging around people of ill-repute and squandering *your* property.

Third, how does the father reward the wasteful prodigal? He kills the fatted calf and throws a party, yet through all these years of faithful obedience, he has never once honored the older son.

Let us flesh this out a bit. The Son initially lived with the Father (as God), had enjoyed full inheritance with a wealthy God. God is indeed wealthy. *The earth is the Lord's and all that it contains.* (1 Cor. 10:26, *para.*) All of creation – plus all of the Father's love and grace – as inheritance belonging to the Son. Yet, Jesus as Son, eschewed

---

[33] Our appreciation of God as triune, the Trinity, evolved and was elucidated only centuries after Jesus told this parable of the Prodigal Son. Jesus as an earthly human being did not view himself as co-eternal with or co-equal to the Father. Hence, this self-understanding of Jesus' being does not do damage to the later theological understanding of the Trinity.

equality with God as something to be exploited; [emptying] himself, taking the form of a slave, born in human likeness. ... (*See generally,* Philippians 2:6-11) He did not keep the inheritance to himself.

And so, the Son left the Father behind, taking with him to a distant land his inheritance of love and grace. He squandered this inheritance on those most unworthy to receive it, the prostitutes, the tax collectors, the sinners, all who were/are in dissolute living, if you will.

Pigs are unclean, and what creatures does the Son find himself living among? Pigs. Tax collectors and sinners. But the Son eventually returned home, as Jesus returned to the Father. Another meal was contemplated, perhaps a heavenly banquet, or perhaps a meal Luke intended as foreshadowing the meal at the end of the Road to Emmaus, an earthly Eucharistic feast. Regardless, the Son returned home to a celebration because, the Father says, *This son of mine was dead, and he has come back to life.* This son of mine was lost, but now is found.

Does it matter whether the story is allegorical more than metaphoric? In every interpretation of the prodigal, this included, the Father is as radical in his welcome of the Son, as the shepherd is in searching out and finding stray sheep, as the radical householder turning her house upside down to find the lost coin. Even more radical is this: the religious leaders, the ones who *do not get it* – are resident in God the Father's house. Always have been. *All I have is yours,* the Father says to the son complaining. Don't you know it?

Only, the Son did not come to save them, but the lost. No, they did not know it. They did not understand. They did not apprehend or appreciate the Gospel of love and grace, yet in what could be one of the greatest ironies in all of Scripture, even the faithful Pharisees are in! The rude, the snippy, the judgmental? God loves and welcomes them, too, the most unlovable of all. *All God has is theirs* ... They just don't get it.

But God is especially fond of those who appear to be the most lost – not just the son, but the sinners with whom he cavorts. In this interpretation, God dispenses the Son to leave the ranch and all the wealth of heaven to come and enmesh himself in the culture of the lost, not just to preach to them from the outside, not just to talk at them or point the way, but to *become one of them*. Didn't Paul also write, *He made him who knew no sin to become sin on our behalf, that we might become the righteousness of God?* How does the Son become sin? How do we become righteousness? Isn't sin an action and righteousness a state of being? There is no physicality to either, yet you and I are physical beings. *Metaphysically* we become righteous while Jesus metaphysically becomes sin, and I cannot understand the mechanics of exchange.

But I do know that the son ate the food of the pigs, and that I have been redeemed. No, I cannot understand the mechanics of exchange, but I can appreciate the charity of exchange.

What I still do not understand, however, is that a shepherd – presumably the Father – would leave the ninety-nine sheep behind in order to seek and save the one most lost, the Pharisee who has no apparent sin? The elder son, the one who scorned the work of the younger, the pompous, pious, arrogant and self-sufficient. Why would God seek to save that one? Leave the ninety-nine sinners in the fold to find the one who not only does not get it, but refuses to get it?

Talk about true love. God loves the Pharisee just as much as God loves me.

Chapter 12

Good Friday: The Irony of the Cross

Holy Week can be exhausting.

In the opening scene to *Fiddler on the Roof*, the family is darting about making frenetic, last minute preparations just before the sun sets to usher in Shabbat. The table must be set, meat cut and cooked, beans buttered, suits and dresses pressed, souls steadied. The preparation is chaotic, up until that very last moment when, right as the sun relinquishes the horizon, and Golde, the mother, lights the candles according to tradition, waves her hands in circlets inward and upward, and apprehends Shabbat on behalf of the family.

The same frenetic energy attends Holy Week preparations. Bulletins are drafted and re-drafted. Ushers are scheduled and rescheduled. Acolytes, too, and the Altar Guild wants to know, *will there be a baptism at this year's Vigil? Where should we place the paschal candle?* Instructions, too, corral volunteers to place extra chairs in the nave, to make coffee and pour champagne, and to hide Easter eggs for children. Clergy renew vows and write sermons.

Simultaneously, the preacher writes homilies or sermons for Maundy Thursday, praying and ruminating about Jesus' last supper, the *institution* of the Eucharist, and Jesus' death, while praying and ruminating about life and resurrection and empty tombs. Life and death engaged simultaneously. The emotional state of the preacher is surreal during Holy Week, like some bizarre compass that points north and south simultaneously, emotionally high one minute, and wallowing in despair the next.

This yo-yo of emotions stresses the physical body to the point of collapse on Easter afternoon. Consequently, most clergy let Easter end on the afternoon of Easter Day, and not the Day of Pentecost (following the Great Fifty Days)! A person can tolerate only so much emotional and physical stress. I know of one priest who died at age forty-nine of a stroke one week after Easter.

Each year, I think to myself, *I'll plan ahead*. And, believe me, I try. I draft bulletins weeks in advance. I write the Easter sermon two or three weeks prior to the day. I visit homebound parishioners and make altar decisions well in advance. And each year, the approach of Holy Week *feels* calm and serene. And each year, I wonder to myself, *Will I make it through unscathed? Can I at least pretend to be Mary rather than Martha?*

On Wednesday of Holy Week several years ago, I thought I had planned well and didn't have much left to do. My friend and parishioner Philip Norris invited me to go on a bike ride with him, so I answered, *Absolutely!* I assumed he meant a relaxed ride around the Tiburon peninsula, which takes about one hour, but he had a more *lofty* goal in mind – Mt. Tam. Mt. Tam rises 2600 feet above sea level, and of course its base is at sea level. Trails and fire roads lead the way up Mt. Tam, which means that making it to the top is neither difficult nor easy. It is, however, time-consuming and exhausting. As we rode to the top, we shared our dreams for the future. The ride *was* both taxing and exhilarating, particularly during Holy Week. Spending time in nature with a friend insulated me from the holy Wednesday of that particular year.

Maundy Thursday, too – I quietly revised my Easter sermon, but I also spent time looking at a Tennessee house online, one I was interested in purchasing as I planned my move home that coming summer. That night, the special St. Stephen's Maundy Thursday *celebration* proved to be less emotional for me than it usually was. Following distribution of the communion bread, and before offering the wine, the St. Stephen's choir typically hosted a light Mediterranean meal around the altar itself. In this liturgy, the congregation *becomes* the disciples, eating hope with Jesus and enjoying one another's company. After the meal is cleared, the blessed wine is offered, the altar stripped, and the old wooden cross moved to the altar steps.

Only this year, I could not remember whether I was supposed extinguish the aumbry candle or leave it lit. I suddenly felt on stage far removed from the deeper spiritual place I like to find myself when stripping the altar. But that was *my* experience, and nobody else seemed to notice.

By the next morning, Good Friday, I felt restored and took a jog with my little dog, twelve-pound Pierre. As we ran, my mind drifted along both worldly and spiritual lines, but I felt little or no emotion.

I mention my emotional state to emphasize that this particular Holy Week was moving along a straight line trajectory, unlike the usual Holy Week emotional roller coaster. The emotional peace lasted until the next day, at the Good Friday service.

Many clergy will tell you that they do not like the arcane *atonement* theory of the cross. According to the atonement theory, Jesus died on the cross in your stead. Your sins are capital, deserving death. The only way to escape punishment is for someone without sin to die in your place. There is, after all, no forgiveness of sin without the shedding of blood, says Scripture. (Heb. 9:22) Jesus, as the only perfect person, is the only one qualified to take your place. Jesus as Son did so at the direction of the Father – and he who knew no sin became sin that you might be forgiven of sin (and avoid capital punishment). (*See* 2 Corin. 5:21)

Paul articulated this atonement theory in his letter to the Romans. You have sinned and fallen short of the glory of God. (Rom. 3:23) The wages of sin is death. (Rom. 6:23) But you are freed from your sin by Jesus Christ. (Rom. 6:22, 23)

Likewise, Isaiah anticipating atonement, described God's *suffering servant* as the one who carries the suffering of others:

> *He was oppressed, and he was afflicted,*
> *yet he did not open his mouth;*
> *like a lamb that is led to the slaughter,*

and like a sheep that before its shearers is silent,
so he did not open his mouth.
…

Yet it was the will of the Lord to crush him with pain.
When you make his life an offering for sin,
he shall see his offspring and shall prolong his day;
through him the will of the Lord shall prosper.
…

he shall bear their iniquities.
…

because he poured himself to death,
and was numbered with the transgressors;
yet he bore the sins of many,
and made intercession for the transgressors.
   -Is. 53:7-12

Jewish tradition holds that God's suffering servant is Israel itself, suffering for the whole world. In one of the more compelling postwar novels I've read, *The Last of the Just,* by Andre Shwarz-Bart, the protagonists are *messianic* Jewish figures born to save each generation. Each *just* person bears pain in the stead of others.

Jesus bore your pain, and carried your affliction. (Is. 53:4)

I suspect most clergy do not like *substitutionary atonement* because, although supremely *just,* it *feels* unjust. That God would establish or create a system in the first place by which blood would need to be shed for forgiveness is confounding, and seems contrary to a god who created us out of love. If God is a father, what father would penalize his child with death because of misbehavior? In most cases, the punishment does not match the crime. Moreover, you and I were born into sin; to the extent there is *original sin,* we had no choice over being born into a broken world in which we have no choice but to sin. *The devil made me do it* is a reality, not just a Flip Wilson punchline. And it seems we are caught in the crossfire of some cosmic war of the gods, one not of our own making. We sin because we cannot *not* sin, a concept that clings to Scripture.

There is so *much* that is wrong with *substitutionary atonement,* and yet, there Jesus is, *The Last of the Just,* dying on the cross in our stead.

And there I was, on that particular Good Friday, listening to the reading from Wisdom, to Psalm 22, and to the lone voice reading the Passion according to John, when finally at the death of Jesus, the reader paused long enough to give us mourners the opportunity to make a pilgrimage from pew to cross, to touch it, or kiss or bow to it, or somehow revere not only the cross, but the passion itself. The passion of the Lord. Being more low-church than high, I had avoided cross veneration throughout my life until now, but someone on staff had suggested we give it a try. I thought, *why not,* so there I was, the first in line. It all felt quite solemn, and I moved to the center, in front of the life-sized wooden cross, rough, hewn, and worn itself, with railroad nails sticking out of the cross ties. I bowed, kissed my hand, then touched the cross. I returned to my pew on the front row and faced forward. I sat eyes closed, then eyes opened, then closed again,

and during that time, I watched as person after person, pilgrim after pilgrim, lined up as if *going up to Jerusalem,* waiting for a turn to venerate. Person after person kissed or touched, or held the arms of the cross. One person kneeled, another bowed, and another just stood there, with eyes open or shut, I cannot know.

My own eyes teared, not because each person was unloading his or her sin onto the back of an innocent Jesus ever on the cross. Rather, each imperfect but truthful person – many of whom I knew personally – each imperfect person with some form of death or loss or disease or dishonesty or irreverence or sin or fault or failure in his or her life – some enormous burden that he or she had carried for days or weeks or years – I watched each person not so much lay the burden down at the foot of a cross for a muscular Jesus to bear, but each person literally walk into the cross. Walk into the cross as though becoming, with his or her burden, some part of Jesus himself, carrying their own crosses.

Each of us became Jesus carrying the cross, suffering on the cross. The body of Christ, not just in glory, but in pain and suffering, with the plight of this world on their backs, becoming impossibly one with Jesus.

Jesus didn't die on the cross, I realized; we died on the cross.

It wasn't that Jesus was substituted for us, it was that Jesus enabled each of us climb onto the cross ourselves. I have been crucified with Christ, and it is no longer I who live, but Christ who lives in me. And the life I now live in the flesh, I live by faith in the Son of God. Who loved me and gave himself up for me. *Or who let me become him.* (*para.* Gal. 2:20)

I suppose all of this might sound offensive or sacrilegious. Heretical, even. Yet, some mystical event took place two thousand years ago by which the burden of humanity was borne on the cross itself. My burden –

And so, you thought it was Jesus who bore humanity, but perhaps Jesus showed us we could bear it by grace. Take up your cross, Jesus said. Thing is, you have been carrying it all along. Time to lay it down.

Epilogue

Attention: Faith, hope and love

On a return trip home several years ago, I suffered a five-hour layover in Chicago. I did what most people do during an airport layover: I walked, read a little, answered email, walked some more, ate a late lunch (or was it an early dinner?), and then walked some more. As I walked through the terminal, I passed the typical airport stores, like a bookstore, Hudson News, an electronics store. *Why do airports have so many electronics stores?* I asked myself. Then Auntie Annie's Pretzels, another Hudson News, and McDonald's.

I was peeking into these stores, people-watching mostly, when I suddenly remembered my mother's birthday. Her birthday had come and gone, and I was late, as usual. I refused to buy some airport tchotchke for her, but I did see an *artsy* store up ahead on the left. I say "artsy" because it called itself "artsy," which is why I had my doubts. I had extra time, so I walked into the store and started reading the store, left to right.

A salesman walked up behind me and asked, *"Having a good day?"*

I answered curtly, *I'm okay, thanks,* and kept my back to him.

I noticed a glass shelf with music box mechanisms on it – the raw mechanism only, without the box. My two kids and I have given these tiny instruments as presents to each other over the years. When you place the mechanism on a solid surface, like a desk, and turn the crank, the desk becomes a sounding board amplifying the mechanism's sound. I considered, *maybe Mom would like one of these the same way the kids and I like them.* I picked one up that played that old Louis Armstrong tune, *What a Wonderful World.*

I see trees of green, and red roses too,
I see them bloom, for me and you ...

and I think to myself,
What a Wonderful World.

Yes, I thought, she would like that. Still moving from left to right, the music mechanism in my hand, I hunted for a second present for Mom. About ten feet away, I noticed a display shelf near the floor holding carved African soapstone. During retirement, Mom raised money for twenty-years to fund orphans' education in Kenya. She would spend months in Kenya each year, and over the years she had more soapstone giraffes and carved wooden elephants than you can possibly imagine. But Mom had grown old, and could no longer make the trip. I thought maybe she might miss going, and wondered if a carving might bring back sweet memories. I noticed a dog carved into one of the dishes ...

Caught up in my own thoughts, I heard the salesman come up behind me again. *"Those are from Kenya."*

I was about to respond curtly a second time, with *"I know, thank you,"* only when I turned to look, it wasn't the salesman, but an older lady. She was a clerk, also, a black woman from the south. I do not know how I mistook her voice for that of a man, but I did. She had a kindly look about her. I had been leaning over to look at the soapstone on the bottom shelf, but now I stood up and answered her square. *"My mom used to go to Kenya."*

"Oh, my," she said. *"Mothers."* Her use of the word, *Mothers*, belied a world of wisdom tucked into the word itself. I asked about her mother. *"Oh, dear, my mother died quite a long time ago."*

"Was she from Chicago?"

"No, no," she answered. *"Mississippi."*

"You grew up in Mississippi?"

"I did, dear, but that was a long time ago. Southern Mississippi. My mom lived there her whole life." She seemed wistful, with chasms of time and space dissipating.

"You miss her."

"I do. Most days. She was the most wonderful woman."
"How so?"

"Well, now. My mother. She was never in a rush. Not like people these days. She gave full attention to whoever she was talking to, however much attention they needed. However much time. Never in a hurry, no, not at all like people today."

This lovely woman gave me her full attention, uncorrupted by discreet motives. People always seem to be in such a rush, talking to one person while planning to talk to someone else. Even texting. It mimics conversations, but how do you explore another person's soul with memes and miniature words? And FaceBook, what an extraordinary tool, but it builds as many walls as it paves roads. I don't like your political views, but I do like the chocolate cake you baked for desert.

This kindly woman was in no hurry at all. In fact, I wondered whether she might have become her mother, giving me her full attention, as in fact she did. *"My mother would go deeper with people, whoever needed her to, and whatever person was standing in front of her, that person received her complete focus."*

"I admire people like that," I responded. She nodded.

I assumed this job was her post-retirement job, so I asked her, "What did you do before you retired?"

"Taught. Children. Young children. Forty years." She may have added, *"special needs children,"* but I don't remember. I do remember thinking, *"This woman gave each child she taught her full attention."* I could tell.

We had moved by now to the counter so I could pay. She was wrapping the soapstone carefully in tissue paper, meditatively. She offered to wrap the raw music box, too, only it wasn't breakable and I told her she didn't need to waste time doing so. But, of course, for this woman, it wouldn't have been a waste of time. For she had learned from her mother, that each person standing in front of her was the only person in her world. This approach to life was inscribed on this woman's soul, learned daily from her mother – the most important person in her life.

In some Jewish families, there is a long tradition of teaching children the Hebrew alphabet early. Maybe an old uncle will carve little blocks of wood into letters. He will make a gift of the blocks, and the toddler at two or three years old will play with the blocks, day in and day out, and chew on the blocks, and build with the blocks, and roll the blocks in dirt and bury them in sand, and treasure the blocks, so much so that even each jot and tittle of the alphabet will become a permanent tattoo on the child's mind, to the point that reading becomes a natural expression.

Over the years, I have visited many people with dementia. Often, these people are so far gone that they no longer recognize their own children. Yet, when I start to say the Lord's Prayer, or the Confession of Sin, or the 23d Psalm – well, some verses are inscribed inside of them, part of their essence, and they will recite verse by verse with me.

In the Sermon on the Mount, Jesus admonished his followers to let their righteousness flourish, to exceed that of the Scribes and Pharisees. Jesus often sounded harsh when speaking of the religious leaders, reproving them for hypocrisy. ... *[Y]ou tithe mint, dill, and cumin, and have neglected the weightier matters of the law: justice and mercy and faith.* (Matt. 23:23)

Yet, the Scribes and Pharisees appeared to be extremely *righteous*. They obeyed the law, and Jesus affirmed the law. He intended to fulfill it, he had said. Not one *jot,* not one apostrophe, must be omitted from the law.

Jesus continued this line of thought by stressing the importance not only of keeping the law, but even the spirit of the law. *You have heard it said ... "you shall not murder" .... But I say to you that if you are angry with a brother or sister, you will be liable to the council ....* (Matt. 5:21,22)

But how is that possible, never to be angry? How is it possible in righteousness to exceed that of the Pharisees and Scribes?

The Pharisees and Scribes paid attention to their actions, to be sure, but to what end? Where was their love? Where was their faith, their spirituality? What was the condition of their souls, as they practiced their righteousness?

Grace has not replaced the law. Grace illuminates the law. Law is important, and life needs a structural framework. Law inscribed onto the soul, repeated over and over to teach us what love and respect and dignity look like.

The Sermon on the Mount appears at first to look like new and improved law that supplants the antique, brittle law of Moses. But Jesus' sermon is not a new law, but an explication of the old law. Love, Jesus says, was required all along, and the law of Moses only ever works as a byproduct of grace.

While the woman in the airport store placed the last of my little presents into a bag, I asked her, *"Why are you working now? You're retired, and I'm guessing on a teacher's pension, so you don't need to work, do you?"*

She hesitated, then said, *"My husband died the day after Thanksgiving,"* two months earlier. *"It's okay. He had cancer, and it was time. And he's with Jesus, now, this I know."*

She never answered my question, not literally. Why was she working? But I knew. She was working through grief. She was working to infuse her life with meaning. To give herself away to others, to me, and to anyone else who happened into that artsy store that held no art. That is who she was, who she is, her character etched onto her soul.

I walked out of the store and down the airport hallway to return to my gate. I grew wistful, and tears filled my eyes. I reflected upon this lovely woman and her kind words and our exchange. I thought of my own mother, who is aging, and all she taught me, and about life and what is important, and especially faith. And I recalled one more time that what seems to be important is usually the red herring, and what is truly important is what I've most often overlooked.

And I thought to myself, *That woman. I've found someone who has fulfilled the law of Moses.*

Most Christians of integrity want to know what will please God.

Hope is the desire to please God, the desire that life will hold meaning, the desire that there is a future.

Faith is the introduction to relationship, the sustenance of relationship, and the flowering of relationship. Faith is gift.

But love. Well, to know one is loved by God and to love God in return, now that rises above all. Love is the pleasing of God, it holds its own meaning, it delivers the future in the present. Love is above all else, relationship, and God as Divine and Jesus as Son – well, all they ever wanted is for us to realize that. To realize each of us is – I am – *loved* completely, and perhaps to respond in kind – with God, and with that person next to me. To give that person all that I am.

And now abide three things. Faith, hope and love. And the greatest of these is love.

www.ingramcontent.com/pod-product-compliance
Lightning Source LLC
Chambersburg PA
CBHW032231080426
42735CB00008B/800